Unfamiliar Fishes

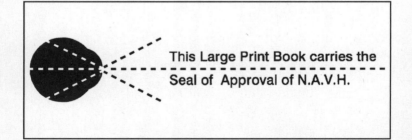

This Large Print Book carries the Seal of Approval of N.A.V.H.

UNFAMILIAR FISHES

SARAH VOWELL

THORNDIKE PRESS
A part of Gale, Cengage Learning

Detroit • New York • San Francisco • New Haven, Conn • Waterville, Maine • London

GALE
CENGAGE Learning

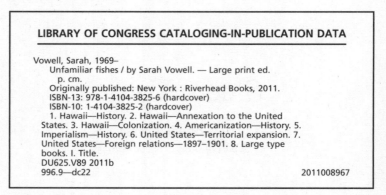

LIBRARY OF CONGRESS CATALOGING-IN-PUBLICATION DATA

Vowell, Sarah, 1969–
   Unfamiliar fishes / by Sarah Vowell. — Large print ed.
   p. cm.
   Originally published: New York : Riverhead Books, 2011.
   ISBN-13: 978-1-4104-3825-6 (hardcover)
   ISBN-10: 1-4104-3825-2 (hardcover)
   1. Hawaii—History. 2. Hawaii—Annexation to the United
States. 3. Hawaii—Colonization. 4. Americanization—History. 5.
Imperialism—History. 6. United States—Territorial expansion. 7.
United States—Foreign relations—1897–1901. 8. Large type
books. I. Title.
DU625.V89 2011b
996.9—dc22   2011008967

Published in 2011 by arrangement with Riverhead Books, a member of Penguin Group (USA), Inc.

Printed in the United States of America
1 2 3 4 5 6 7 15 14 13 12 11

TO OWEN

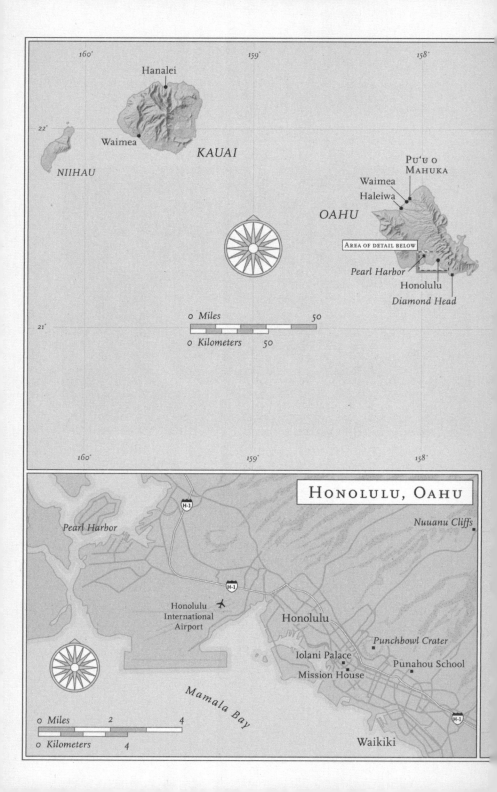

160°   159°   158°

Hanalei

22°

Waimea

KAUAI

NIIHAU

Pu'u o
Mahuka

Waimea

Haleiwa

OAHU

AREA OF DETAIL BELOW

21°

Pearl Harbor

Honolulu

Diamond Head

o *Miles*   50

o *Kilometers*   50

160°   159°   158°

HONOLULU, OAHU

H-1

Pearl Harbor

Nuuanu Cliffs

H-1

Honolulu
International
Airport

Honolulu

Punchbowl Crater

Iolani Palace

Mission House

Punahou School

Mamala Bay

H-1

o *Miles*   2   4

o *Kilometers*   4

Waikiki

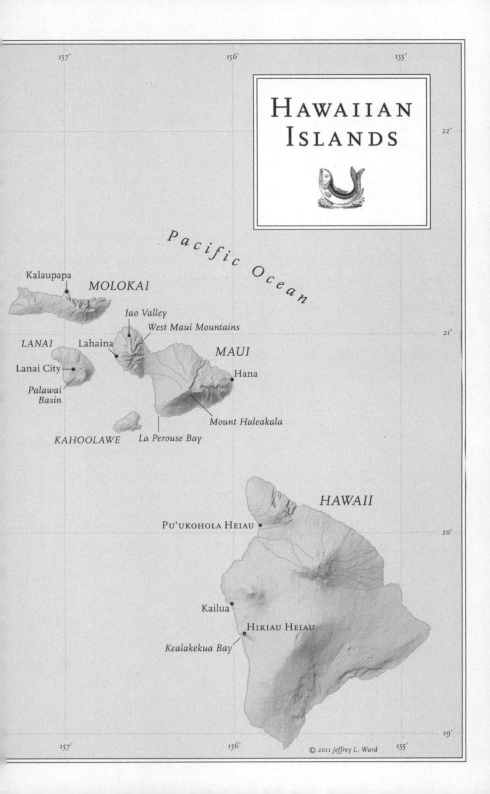

HAWAIIAN ISLANDS

Pacific Ocean

Kalaupapa

MOLOKAI

Iao Valley

West Maui Mountains

LANAI   Lahaina   MAUI

Lanai City   Hana

Palawai
Basin

KAHOOLAWE   La Perouse Bay

Mount Haleakala

HAWAII

Pu'ukohola Heiau

Kailua

Hikiau Heiau

Kealakekua Bay

© 2011 Jeffrey L. Ward

A NOTE ON THE TEXT

While I have retained some Hawaiian diacritical marks I believe English readers will find helpful in navigating oceans of vowels, in "Nahiʻenaʻena" for instance, I have dispensed with them in other words common in English usage or Hawaiian history, referring to the state that is the book's subject as "Hawaii" rather than "Hawaiʻi," or the residence of the Kalakaua dynasty as "Iolani" Palace rather than " ʻIolani," or the last Hawaiian queen as "Liliuokalani" rather than "Liliʻuokalani," etc.

The land we live in seems to be strong and active. But how fares the land that lives in us?
— GROVER CLEVELAND, "Patriotism and Holiday Observance"

In the morning there was a big wind blowing and the waves were running high up on the beach and he was awake a long time before he remembered that his heart was broken.
— ERNEST HEMINGWAY, "Ten Indians"

Why is there a glop of macaroni salad next to the Japanese chicken in my plate lunch? Because the ship *Thaddeus* left Boston Harbor with the first boatload of New England missionaries bound for Hawaii in 1819. That and it's Saturday. Rainbow Drive-In only serves *shoyu* chicken four days a week.

A banyan tree in Waikiki is a fine spot for a sunburned tourist from New York City to sit beneath and ponder the historical implications of a lukewarm box of takeout. Because none of us belong here — not me, not the macaroni, not the chicken soaked in soy sauce, not even the tree.

Like a lot of people and things in these islands, banyans are imports from somewhere else. In this case, India. The banyan's gray branches shoot off slim sprouts that drip down and bore slowly into the ground and take root, bulging into new, connected trunks so as to support more and more tendrils, leading to more and more trunks, until each tree becomes its own spooky little forest.

There is a banyan shading Courthouse Square in the town of Lahaina, on Maui, that was planted in 1873 to commemorate the fiftieth anniversary of the arrival of New England missionaries on that island. It was eight feet tall when a missionary descendant planted it, and now it stands over sixty feet high, with twelve trunks spanning more than two hundred square feet.

One time I was in the Lahaina courthouse chatting with a woman who worked there about the banyan. She told me that the town gardeners put a lot of effort into confining that tree within the square because otherwise it would keep on growing until its roots and branches cracked the foundations and punctured the walls of all the nearby buildings, finally toppling everything in its path. In fact, the banyan's tendency to crowd out and destroy its neighbors has earned it the pet name "strangler fig."

Here in Waikiki, the U.S. Army Museum is hunkered down in the midst of all the concrete high-rise hotels and condominiums built in the post-1959 statehood architectural style I like to think of as A Very Brady

Brutalism. The park where my plate lunch and I are sitting appears in an old black-and-white photograph on display there. The picture was taken in the summer of 1898, a few days after the sons of missionaries who had dethroned the Hawaiian queen handed over Hawaii to the United States. The park is pitched with the tents of the First New York Voluntary Infantry. The Spanish-American War had the soldiers stopping off in this suddenly American city en route to the Philippines to persuade the Filipino people at gunpoint that self-government really isn't for everyone. They named their encampment after the president who dispatched them here: Camp McKinley.

The United States declared war on Spain in April of 1898. By August, the McKinley administration had invaded the Spanish colonies of Cuba, Puerto Rico, the Philippines, and Guam and annexed Hawaii. In this four-month orgy of imperialism, the United States became a world power for the first time — became what it is now.

"Hurrah for Hawaii!" Theodore Roosevelt wrote from Cuba when he heard the news that the U.S. annexed the islands. He was in the Caribbean with the Rough Riders, licking the Spanish at Santiago de Cuba. One of the end results of that conquest was

American control of Guantánamo Bay. To Roosevelt and his likeminded cronies in the government and military, the most important objective of all the 1898 maneuvers was possession of far-flung islands for naval bases at strategic ports like Guantanámo and Honolulu's Pearl Harbor. He and his friends had pined for these bases for years the way a normal man envisions his dream house. All they ever wanted was a cozy little global empire with a few islands here and there to park a fleet of battleships.

That Japanese dive-bombers sank four of those battleships in Pearl Harbor on December 7, 1941, is how I ended up getting interested in Hawaii in the first place a few years back. The purpose of my initial visit was a quick jaunt to see the USS *Arizona* Memorial, the monument in the harbor perched above the oily, watery grave of the 1,177 sailors who died on the ship that day. Unlike the flip-flop wearers on my flight to Honolulu, I didn't come here for direct sunlight or "fun." I came to Hawaii because it had been attacked.

After I checked the *Arizona* off my to-do list, I still had some time to kill. So I swung by the Iolani Palace downtown, curious to take a look at the Victorian building my guidebook billed as the "only palace in the

United States."

A guide led my tour group into the room where the white businessmen and sugar planters who had staged a coup d'état against Queen Liliuokalani in 1893 locked her up for treason after her royalist supporters botched a counterrevolution.

Liliuokalani whiled away her imprisonment in a room on the second floor of the palace, renamed the "Executive Building," sewing a colorful quilt that is on display there. Perhaps out of melancholy — or spite — little flags of the Kingdom of Hawaii stand guard around the quilt's center square. In one corner she embroidered a scene of a cartoonish man struggling with an umbrella, losing his hat in the wind. The guide chuckled over this quaint bit of slapstick, but I wondered if it was the sly lament of a woman whose crown has blown away and it isn't coming back.

I should mention that I was there in December of 2003. The week before I arrived in Honolulu, American soldiers captured Saddam Hussein, who was hiding in his grungy spider hole outside of Tikrit. So when I was standing in the Victorian-era cell of a Polynesian queen deposed by the sons of churchy New Englanders, at that exact moment the Iraqi dictator was behind

19

bars in a U.S. military compound being guarded by Pennsylvanians. Not that the queen, a constitutional monarch and accomplished musician famous for writing the love song "Aloha 'Oe," and Saddam, a mass murderer famous for gassing five thousand Kurds, had much in common. Still, there's an identifiable link between the two overthrows, an American tendency to indulge in what trendy government lingo at the time was calling "regime change."

When the Iolani Palace tour guide mentioned the day the Hawaiian flag on the palace grounds was lowered and the American flag went up, she looked like she was going to cry. I couldn't help but picture that scene from the TV news earlier in the year when a U.S. soldier celebrated the invasion of Baghdad by climbing up a statue of Saddam and covering his bronze mustachioed face with the Stars and Stripes, a gesture that was both unfortunate as PR and improper flag etiquette.

It was telling to spend the morning at a historic site like Pearl Harbor — one tattooed on the American memory — and the afternoon at another historic site we have forgotten entirely. In light of the then-current events, I wasn't sure whether to be comforted or dismayed. The groundswell of

20

outrage over the invasion of Iraq often cited the preemptive war as a betrayal of American ideals. The subtext of the dissent was: *This is not who we are.* But not if you were standing where I was. It was hard to see the look in that palace tour guide's eyes when she talked about the American flag flying over the palace and not realize that ever since 1898, from time to time, this is exactly who we are. And what's more, Hawaii is, just as Theodore Roosevelt's circle predicted, crucial to the American empire's military presence in the Pacific. Pearl Harbor is still the headquarters of U.S. Pacific Command, just as it was for all three of America's twentieth-century wars in the Pacific with Japan, North Korea, and North Vietnam.

So I started looking into Hawaii's bit part in the epic of American global domination. I came across a political cartoon on the cover of *Harper's Weekly* from August 27, 1898. Above the caption "Uncle Sam's New Class in the Art of Self-Government," Uncle Sam poses as a schoolmaster in a classroom festooned with a world map in which little American flags are planted on the barely visible island dots of Guam, Hawaii, Puerto Rico, Cuba, and the Philippines. A barefoot, frowning boy wearing a dunce cap labeled

"Aguinaldo" represents the Filipino revolutionary who began the Spanish-American War as an American ally against Spain; but after Spain surrendered and handed over the Philippines to the United States, Aguinaldo led the guerilla war against his new American colonizers. Uncle Sam is trying to break up a fight between two other barefoot boys, one wearing a satchel marked "Cuban Ex-Patriot" and the other a belt marked "Guerilla" meant to symbolize the unruly discontentment of Cuban freedom fighters also dismayed that their American allies in the fight against Spain for *Cuba libre* had just become their new colonial overlord. Meanwhile, off to the side, two good little girls, their headdresses identifying them as "Hawaii" and "Porto Rico," have their noses in the books they are quietly reading. Presumably because well-behaved Hawaii and Puerto Rico have politely and graciously accepted the blessings of annexation without any back talk.

This book tells the story of how that perception came to be, how Americans and their children spent the seventy-eight years between the arrival of Protestant missionaries in 1820 and the American annexation in 1898 Americanizing Hawaii, importing our favorite religion, capitalism, and our second-favorite religion, Christianity. It is also the story of how Hawaiians withstood these changes, and how the Hawaiian ruling class willingly participated in the process.

Before the white revolutionaries overthrew the queen with the help of U.S. Marines in 1893, the preceding decades provide a de facto case study in what the political scientist Steven Lukes called soft power, the process by which one people gets another group of people "to want what you want." In this case, American missionaries, as well as their frequent foes and fellow Americans, the commercial sailors, inspired the Hawaiians to want money, education, constitutional government, Christian salvation, and Western material goods. After the United States Minister to Hawaii conspired with the missionary boys in the overthrow of the queen, he reported to Washington, "The Hawaiian pear is now fully ripe, and this is the golden hour for the United States to pluck it."

In certain ways, the Americanization of Hawaii in the nineteenth century parallels the Americanization of America. Just as their Puritan forebears had set off on their errand into the wilderness of New England, the New England missionaries set sail for the Sandwich Islands, a place they thought

23

of as a spiritual wilderness. Just as perhaps nine out of ten natives of the Americas were wiped out by contact with European diseases, so was the native Hawaiian population ravaged by smallpox, measles, whooping cough, and venereal disease. Just as the Industrial Revolution and the building of the railroads brought in the huddled masses of immigrants to the United States, the sugar plantations founded by the sons of the missionaries required massive imports of labor, primarily from China, Japan, Korea, Portugal, and the Philippines, transforming Hawaii into what it has become, a multiethnic miscellany in which every race is a minority.

Hence the plate lunch. Two scoops of Japanese-style rice and one scoop of macaroni salad seemingly airlifted from some church potluck in Anywhere, U.S.A., are served alongside a Polynesian or Asian protein such as *kalua* pig, chicken *adobo, teriyaki* beef, or Loco Moco (a hamburger patty topped with gravy and a fried egg, a dish presumably invented to remedy what has always been the hamburger's most obvious defect — not enough egg).

Sugar plantation workers used to share food at lunchtime, swapping tofu and Chinese noodles for Korean spareribs and

Portuguese bread. That habit of hodgepodge got passed down, evolving into the plate lunch now served at diners, drive-ins, and lunch trucks throughout the Hawaiian archipelago.

In 1961, the late Seiju Ifuku established the Rainbow Drive-In, the joint on the edge of Waikiki where I bought my plate lunch. Ifuku had been an army cook with the One Hundredth Infantry Battalion. The mostly Hawaii-born Japanese-American volunteer soldiers in the One Hundredth and the 442nd Regimental Combat Team served as segregated troops in Europe and North Africa during World War II, becoming the most decorated unit in U.S. military history and earning the nickname the "Purple Heart Battalion." Their motto was "Remember Pearl Harbor." Their argument was that they were Americans, not, as the U.S. government classified them and their families, "enemy aliens."

Rainbow Drive-In's menu, offering teriyaki, hot dogs, mahimahi, and Portuguese sausage, reads like a list of what America is supposed to be like — a neighborly mishmash. Barack Obama, the Honolulu-born president of the United States, mentioned once on a trip home his craving for plate lunch, listing Rainbow

25

Drive-In as a possible stop. Makes sense, considering that his Kansan mother met his Kenyan father at the University of Hawaii and his mother's remarriage blessed him with a half-Indonesian sister. He's our first plate-lunch president.

I suppose the double-sided way I see the history of Hawaii — as a painful tale of native loss combined with an idealistic multiethnic saga symbolized by mixed plates in which soy sauce and mayonnaise peacefully coexist and congeal — tracks with how I see the history of the United States in general. I am the descendant of Cherokees who were marched at gunpoint by the U.S. Army to Oklahoma on the Trail of Tears. (Incidentally, the Cherokees were Christianized and educated by the American Board of Commissioners for Foreign Missions, the very same New England organization that Christianized and educated the Hawaiians.) Yet I am also, and mostly, the descendant of European immigrants, notably Swedish peasants who left for Kansas for the same reasons Asian and Portuguese plantation workers sailed to Hawaii.

Whenever I eat plate lunch, I always think back to the lore of my Swedish great-grandfather's voyage across the Atlantic. Supposedly, the only food he brought with him on the ship was a big hunk of cheese. Then he befriended a German in steerage whose only food was a big hunk of sausage. The Swede shared his cheese with the German and the German shared his sausage with the Swede.

Growing up, I came to know America as two places — a rapacious country built on the destruction of its original inhabitants, and a welcoming land of opportunity and generosity built by people who shared their sausage and their cheese.

In 1899, the British poet Rudyard Kipling published his famous poem "The White Man's Burden," about the new American empire of island colonies of "new-caught, sullen peoples." Four years earlier, when Kipling visited Washington, D.C., for the first time, he met Theodore Roosevelt. Roosevelt dragged Kipling to the Smithsonian to show off glass cases full of American Indian artifacts. Kipling later wrote, "I never got over the wonder of a people who, having extirpated the aboriginals of their continent more completely than any modern race had ever done, honestly believed that they were a godly little New England community, setting examples to brutal mankind."

Of the five countries the United States

invaded and/or acquired in 1898, Hawaii is the only one that became a state. That said, I have come to understand that even though Hawaii has been a state since 1959 and an American territory since 1898, a small but defiant network of native activists question the legality of both developments and do not consider themselves to be Americans at all. Which is pretty easy to pick up on when they're marching past you down the main drag of Honolulu on the fiftieth anniversary of statehood, carrying picket signs that say "We Are Not Americans."

Hawaiians have a word for all the pasty-faced explorers, Bible thumpers, whalers, tycoons, con men, soldiers, and vacationers who have washed ashore since Captain Cook named their homeland the Sandwich Islands in 1778: *haole.*

Like many nouns in the Hawaiian language, haole evokes multiple meanings, including foreigner, tourist, Caucasian, or, in the movie in which I first learned it, blond nitwit who learned to surf in a suburb of Phoenix.

In 1987 I saw an endearing, low-budget coming-of-age picture about a surfer. In his review of the film, *North Shore,* Vincent Canby of the *New York Times* complained that "the surfing, writing, direction and performances are of a caliber to interest only undiscriminating adolescents." Being seventeen at the time, I liked it. Not being seventeen anymore, I still do. Despite the soundtrack's dated synthesizer shenanigans, there's something sweet and timeless about the protagonist's quest for knowledge and new friends.

Rick, played by Matt Adler, is an amiable, landlocked teenager who surfs in a wave tank in the Arizona desert. When he wins a contest at this motorized bathtub, an announcer asks him, without irony, "How does it feel to be the best surfer in the state of Arizona?"

Rick uses his prize money to fly to Oahu to surf the big waves at the North Shore. Upon arrival, he falls for a native Hawaiian girl named Kiani while studying the path of the "soul surfer" under the tutelage of Chandler, a guru who owns a surf shop. Chandler assigns Rick to work his way through a historical survey of boards, including a thick slab of koa wood used by the ancient Hawaiian surf riders who perfected the sport. Rick discovers, the hard way, underwater hazards unheard of back home in the wave tank. A reef shreds his back, thereby furnishing a romantic yet educational opportunity for the girl he has a crush on to school him in native healing. Kiani soothes his scrapes with a sprig of aloe even though he is wary of antiseptic that doesn't come out of an FDA-approved plastic tube. Through all these tutorials Rick discovers what I would one day find out for myself: in Hawaii, there is so much to learn.

Kiani takes Rick for a walk to a stone *heiau,* or temple, what she calls "an ancient sacred place" built by "priest kings" uphill from Waimea Bay. She shows him how to make a wish by wrapping a lava rock inside a leaf and placing it on the ruins. He's a teenage boy, she's pretty, and it's about to rain; if I've guessed his wish correctly, it almost comes true in the next scene. Too bad the lovers are interrupted by wild-pig hunters — that old teen-movie cliché.

The girlfriend's male relatives are less hospitable to Rick, but when isn't that true? To Kiani's cousin and his tight-knit gang of local surfers committed to defending their home turf from a never-ending flood of yahoos on vacation, Rick personifies two centuries of trespassing. He is oblivious to his status among the locals as a stand-in for every freckled missionary's son who helped turn land into real estate.

This gang is identified as the *hui,* which is

the Hawaiian word for club or organization. Da Hui is a real and formidable surf collective on the North Shore, famous for organizing an annual beach cleanup and for having an attitude that might be politely described as self-assured. The punk band the Offspring once recorded a funny portrait of what it's like to enter their territory, sung from the point of view of a haole who knows his place: "I won't park next to Da Hui/ Because I don't really feel comfortable!"

When Rick meets this daunting crew, he's on his surfboard, bobbing in the sea, just thrilled to be in water that didn't come out of an Arizona faucet.

"Hey, haole," says one of the hui who paddles out to intimidate Rick.

"Hi," a grinning Rick replies, "haole to you too!"

"He's so haole he doesn't even know he's haole," the local informs his friends. Then he advises Rick to scram: "This is our wave."

Admittedly, this is a not-so-major motion picture with the production values of a Bananarama video, but the serious resentment lurking in those words — *this is our wave* — gets to the heart of the whole history of Hawaii's losing battle to ward off foreign intruders.

Rick's uncomfortable run-in is not unprecedented on the North Shore. This information isn't in the movie, but that Waimea heiau he visited with Kiani is a specific kind of temple, one where human sacrifice was practiced centuries ago. It's called Pu'u o Mahuka. The cold shoulder Rick got from those surfers was nothing compared to how their ancestors greeted four sailors from George Vancouver's Royal Navy supply ship, *Daedalus,* when they came ashore for water in 1792. Only one of those men made it back to the ship alive. The three murdered seamen may have been sacrificed at the temple, perhaps on the very rock that Rick wrapped in a leaf, praying to ancient gods that his girlfriend would let him round third base.

I visited the ruins of that temple, which is now maintained by the National Park Service. It commands an otherworldly view of the Waimea Valley and the island's coast. But the most memorable thing to see there might be a plaque the park service erected in 1965 purporting that "this site possesses exceptional value in commemorating and illustrating the history of the United States." My Hawaiian friend who drove me there pointed at this plaque and rolled her eyes.

It is laughable to think that a lava rock temple — built at least a century before the

Declaration of Independence was signed five thousand miles away — has much to do with the history of the United States. (Though it is entertaining to wonder what John Adams would make of the sacrificial demands of ferocious priest kings, given all that fuss about Parliament taxing tea.)

In January of 1778, when George Washington's army was holed up and shivering at Valley Forge, Captain James Cook of the British Royal Navy became the first European on record to set foot in the Hawaiian archipelago, landing at Waimea on the island of Kauai. The seven inhabited Hawaiian islands — Kauai, Oahu, Maui, Molokai, Lanai, Niihau, and Hawaii (also called the Big Island, for obvious reasons) — were governed as separate though interrelated feudalistic chiefdoms. The nephew of one of those ruling high chiefs, the warrior Kamehameha, may have been one of the Big Island natives who clobbered Cook during the confusing scuffle when the explorer got himself killed in 1779 at Kealakekua Bay. Cook and his men attempted to recover a stolen boat by trying to take the high chief hostage. This was, needless to say, frowned upon. The Hawaiians stopped the Brits from kidnapping their chief, and when Cook turned to retreat, natives hit and stabbed him, "his face," a shipmate wrote, "falling into the water."

I have a friend whose father, a native of Liverpool, refused to eat pineapples his entire life because he held a grudge against Hawaiians for killing Britain's greatest explorer.

Three years after Cook's death, Kamehameha's uncle the high chief died. In the ensuing power struggle, Kamehameha had his rival (and cousin) whacked and assumed control of the Big Island. He began acquiring guns, ammunition, a cannon, and a pair of haole advisors from the Western ships that followed in Cook's wake, using them to wage civil wars against the neighboring islands.

Captain George Vancouver had served as a midshipman on Cook's Pacific voyages. When he returned to Hawaii in 1793 at the helm of his own naval expedition, he was alarmed by the devastation. He wrote that "[Maui] and its neighboring islands were reduced to great indigence by the wars in which they had for many years been engaged."

I visited Iao Valley, the site of Maui's bloodiest skirmish, with my sister and nephew. This cool, verdant retreat is one of the most glorious places in the Hawaiian

Islands, which is saying something. A clear creek ambles beside a skinny peak, the Iao Needle, thrusting up more than two thousand feet from the valley floor. I might describe the Needle as adorable, though apparently the ancients regarded it as the phallic stone of Kanaloa, the god of the underworld.

A sign states, "During periods of warfare, the peak was used as a lookout by warriors." I don't know what the lookouts shouted down in 1790 when they saw Kamehameha and his cannon coming but I'm guessing it was the Hawaiian equivalent of *Run for your lives.*

"What's a musket?" my nephew Owen asks me, looking at one of the signs explaining that this was the first big battle of the Hawaiian civil wars to use Western weaponry.

"It's a big, long gun," I tell him. "George Washington's soldiers were using them around the same time as Kamehameha."

Owen, who is eight, knows who Kamehameha is. In fact, he does an amusing if insensitive impression of the Hawaiian warrior. He strips down, twisting his underwear into a loincloth. Brandishing an imaginary spear, he screws his eyes into a menacing stare while shouting, "I'm Kamehameha,

35

and you are going to die!"

We mosey around the valley a little and he points to the creek below the trail. "That's a pretty stream," he says.

I tell him that the battle here in 1790 became known as "the Damming of the Waters" because Kamehameha's muskets and cannon butchered so many of Maui's soldiers that stacks of corpses formed a human dam that stopped up the creek.

Kalanikupule, the Maui commander, escaped the carnage at Iao Valley, but he and Kamehameha would meet again five years later on Oahu, in the Battle of Nuuanu, Kamehameha's last.

Nuuanu is another good view with a bad massacre. These are the cliffs overlooking present-day Honolulu, their serrated edges usually softened in a silvery mist. Kamehameha's forces pursued the enemy warriors up the comely cliffs — and over, a long drop. Around four hundred soldiers were pushed off the peaks.

These are the same rainy cliffs Queen Liliuokalani alludes to in her song "Aloha 'Oe." She had been on a horseback ride over the mountains and noticed one of her friends kissing his girlfriend goodbye. She set to music the story of their romantic farewell. Their "fond embrace" happened to take place on slopes that, decades earlier, had been crucial in Kamehameha's founding of the monarchy Liliuokalani would soon inherit, a scene of such slaughter it's a wonder the lovers in her song didn't trip over a pile of skulls.

Kamehameha conquered all the islands except Kauai (though Kauai eventually, and wisely, submitted to him without a fight). In 1810 he founded the Kingdom of Hawaii and would rule as its first monarch until his death in 1819, missing the first New England missionaries' arrival by mere months.

When Hawaiians describe Kamehameha's path to power, they usually say that he "united" the islands instead of saying that he "conquered" them. That is because islanders had already been fighting civil wars for at least a century before he was born. The ferocity of Kamehameha's battles was matched only by the finality of the peace accompanying his domination. The end result was not unlike that of the Hundred Years' War waged in medieval France — a rickety mishmash of fiefdoms controlled by regional aristocrats giving way to a strong central monarchy and a new sense of national pride.

Kamehameha is so beloved that his birthday is an annual Hawaiian holiday, featuring parades on most of the islands. In a yearly ceremony at the statue of Kamehameha in downtown Honolulu, the fire department backs a fire engine up next to the sculpture and a couple of firefighters spend an hour or so going up and down on a crane, accepting leis from civic organizations and draping them around the king's bronze neck, as if he were on fire and only yellow flower necklaces can put it out.

One year at the lei ceremony, the minister from the church founded by the first missionaries said a prayer. He prefaced his prayer by remarking that Kamehameha united the islands in time for the missionaries to unite them in Christ.

This power shift from a king beholden to the war god Ku to the haole nerds representing the Prince of Peace was inspired by the first Hawaiian Christian, an orphan whose parents were killed by Kamehameha's warriors in a stint of vigorous "uniting."

Opukaha'ia was born on the Big Island around 1792. The haoles called him "Henry Obookiah," and that is how he signed his name once they taught him to write. I will use his anglicized name because I like how it has the word "book" in it. Published in New England in 1818 right after Obookiah died, the slim volume *Memoirs of Henry*

Obookiah launched the first missionaries from Boston Harbor to the Sandwich Islands the following year, or, as one of them described their destination, "the far distant land of Obookiah."

Memoirs of Henry Obookiah and Alfred Thayer Mahan's 1890 colonialism starter-kit, *The Influence of Sea Power upon History,* are arguably the two books published in the nineteenth century that had the most impact on the history of Hawaii. The former summoned American missionaries; the latter beckoned the U.S. military. As Mahan, the godfather of American imperialism circa 1898, would argue in a later, less action-packed, book on religion, "However men severally may regard imperialism as a political theory, the dominion of Christ is essentially imperial, one Sovereign over many communities, who find their oneness in Him, their Ruler."

Obookiah, the young man who invited the army of Christ to invade his homeland, had witnessed Kamehameha's men slaying his parents when he was around ten years old. He tried to escape from their attackers, carrying his infant brother on his back. The pursuers killed the baby with a spear while Henry was still shouldering him.

"I was left alone without father and

mother in this wilderness world," Obookiah would later recall. A child does not have to endure such horror to grow up to be a religious fanatic, but I suppose it helps.

Obookiah went to live with his uncle, a priest at Kealakekua Bay. This is the inlet on the Big Island's west coast where Captain Cook had been killed in 1779. Cook had visited Obookiah's uncle's temple, the Kikiau heiau. In fact, it was where the captain performed the first Christian service in Hawaiian history, a funeral for a member of his crew.

The Kikiau temple was dedicated to Lono, the god of agriculture and peace. Some Hawaiians initially believed Cook to be an incarnation of Lono because his ships resembled the god's symbol and the expedition first arrived in Kauai at the beginning of the Makahiki festival, the annual season of peace devoted to Lono worship, when Ku the war god disappears.

At Kealakekua Bay, the white obelisk erected by British sailors in Cook's honor is visible from the ruins of Obookiah's uncle's temple. The monument and the roped-off patch of grass around it is sovereign British soil. There's also a small marker at the water's edge marking the spot where Cook "met his death."

There are three ways to get to it — swim or kayak from the dock down the shore next to the old temple, or, for us landlubbers, a sweaty, four-hour-roundtrip hike down an overgrown trail from the top of the cliffs above the bay, perhaps with a whiny child in tow. Owen so detested trudging down this unkempt path with me that every subsequent hike we have taken together prompts the following exchange.

Owen: Check if we can kayak instead.
Me: To the top of a mountain?
Him: Just check.

Western ships started rolling in after Cook's findings put the Sandwich Isles on European maps, and Henry Obookiah would sail away on one of them. In *Memoirs,* Obookiah recalls, "While I was with my uncle, for some time I began to think about leaving that country to go to some other part of the globe. I did not care where I shall go to."

Obookiah signed on as a hand on a trading ship out of New York. He did not know then that he had just steered a course for the Second Great Awakening by way of the China trade. The ship left for the Seal Islands between Alaska and Japan to pick

41

up a cargo of sealskins, and then on to Macao, where it was detained by a British warship, proceeding to Canton to trade the sealskins for cinnamon, silk, and tea before returning to New York around the Cape of Good Hope.

In New York, Obookiah disembarked with Thomas Hopu, a Hawaiian shipmate he had met on board. As the missionary Hiram Bingham described their first night in Manhattan, "Like the mass of foreign seamen who then visited our cities without being improved in their morals, [they] were for a time exposed to the evil of being confirmed in vice and ignorance, and in utter contempt of the claims of Christianity." That is how a missionary describes the fact that the Hawaiians went to the theater.

When some New Yorkers invited the Hawaiians to their home, Obookiah recalled, "I thought while in the house of these two gentlemen how strange to see females eat with them."

In Hawaii, it was forbidden — *kapu* — for men and women to eat together. Women were also barred from eating certain foods, notably bananas because the sight of females consuming phallic fruit offended Hawaiian men. Breaking a kapu was a crime, often punishable by death. (After Obookiah's parents were killed, his aunt was executed for a kapu infraction. She was thrown off some cliffs, and her jinxed little nephew saw the whole thing.)

The captain of Obookiah's ship came from New Haven, Connecticut. He invited the boy home with him, and Henry started hanging around the Yale campus. In the tall-tale version of what happened to Obookiah at Yale, he was sitting in a doorway, weeping because unlike the students stepping over him he did not know how to read. Really, he just struck up a conversation with young do-gooder Edwin W. Dwight, who offered to teach the boy to read and write.

Edwin introduced Obookiah to his cousin, Timothy Dwight, the president of Yale, who invited Henry to live in his home. Timothy Dwight was Jonathan Edwards's grandson. If Edwards, author of the 1741 slasher sermon "Sinners in the Hands of an Angry God," had been the idol of the Great Awakening, Timothy Dwight was the biggest star of its sequel, the so-called Second Great Awakening.

"Pope Timothy," as he was nicknamed, assumed the presidency of the college in 1795. Yale was founded by finicky Protestants who worried that the Puritans at Harvard weren't puritanical enough. But the

Revolutionary War brought the Age of Reason to New Haven, and Dwight inherited a student body full of deist beatniks on the Enlightenment highway to hell, which is to say, France. This generation did not just read Voltaire; they literally addressed each other as "Voltaire" the way kids today call one another dude. Like, "Voltaire, I'm so high right now."

Dwight had already published, anonymously, an epic poem narrated by the Devil. Satan dedicated the book to "Mons. de Voltaire" to thank him for teaching "that the chief end of man was to slander his god and abuse him forever."

As Yale's president, professor, and minister, Dwight spent the next few years in the classroom and the pulpit ranting against the European empirical thought that had been "vomited upon us," lecturing on such topics as "The Nature and Danger of Infidel Philosophy." As an author, he was no Grandpa Edwards, but he was eloquent and stubborn and sufficiently terrifying; all that burning-in-hell-forever stuff pretty much writes itself. Eventually the students abandoned France, that "suburb to the world of perdition," returning their hearts home to New England, their ancestral city on a hill.

In 1802, the school trembled with revival.

"Yale College is a little temple," a student wrote his mother.

"It was like a mighty rushing wind," a graduate recalled of the year the revival hit. "The whole college was shaken. It seemed for a time as if the whole mass of the students would press into the kingdom."

As Timothy Dwight's sermons are whipping up yet another revival in 1808, Henry Obookiah is sailing from his uncle's temple at Kealakekua Bay toward the little temple of Yale. Let's pause a moment while Obookiah is still unloading crates of sealskins in the Pacific because I have a thing or two I want to unload myself.

One counterintuitive result of pondering the legacy of New England missionaries in Hawaii is being reminded of how much I used to enjoy studying eighteenth-century France. On one of my trips to Maui, I went to La Perouse Bay, a rocky bit of shoreline at the end of the road on the south coast. Though Captain Cook had sailed past Maui, he had not set foot on it. The first recorded European to do that was Frenchman Jean-François de Galaup, comte de La Pérouse, in 1786. Poking around spiky lava fields that had dribbled down from the last eruption of the Haleakala volcano, I asked a park ranger who happened by if he could tell me anything about Admiral La Pérouse.

"Yes," he said. "He was French."

Wanting a pinch more detail, I went home and started reading up on the expedition, how Louis XVI had commissioned La Pérouse to sail to the Pacific, fine-tune Captain Cook's maps, scope out new trade routes, and bring along an astronomer, a geologist, a botanist, and illustrators to collect specimens and record scientific data. I was especially entranced by the name of one of the frigates under the admiral's command, the *Astrolabe.* Its namesake is a scientific instrument used to calculate the position of stars — very early Captain Cook.

Britain's Royal Society had dispatched Cook, La Pérouse's predecessor and idol, on his first Pacific expedition in time to make it to Tahiti by June 3, 1769, so as to observe the transit of Venus across the sun. That's why they sent him there: to sail for eight months just to catch a glimpse of another planet's orbit, an event that, incidentally, lasted all of six hours. The expedition's calculations were to be used to measure the universe, but since such calculations would not really be accurate until the invention of photography, Cook completed his task yet still sort of failed.

On the bright side, on the way home Cook

stumbled onto New Zealand. Setting forth to learn one thing, he and his shipmates gained extra understanding, and not just that Tahiti might be more beautiful than a speck of another planet loping through the sky. The crew spent weeks there, setting up to observe the transit. In that time, they hung around natives, picked up some of the language, and just generally soaked up a little of the island's way of life. When they arrived in Aotearoa, aka New Zealand, the Tahitian chief who came along for the ride could communicate with the Maori because of the similarities in the two Polynesian languages. Cook returned to Tahiti on his second and third voyages to the Pacific. So when he first sailed into the harbor at Waimea, on Kauai, in 1778 he and his men could communicate on a rudimentary level with the Hawaiians because the language, one of the expedition's surgeons wrote, was "much the same as that of [Tahiti]." This led to one of Cook's most intriguing insights, the identification of what is now called the Polynesian Triangle, that immense stretch of ocean between New Zealand, Easter Island, and Hawaii — including Samoa, Tonga, and Tahiti — with related dialects and customs.

For instance, the New Zealand natives call

themselves Maori, while native Hawaiians' name for themselves is Kanaka Maoli. "Same language, same people, same culture," the Hawaiian activist Kekuni Blaisdell told me.

Cook asked, "How shall we account for this Nation spreading itself so far over this Vast ocean?" Answer: the ancient Polynesians were some of the most skilled and talented natural-born navigators the world has ever known. Which is how the natives of Tahiti and the Marquesas settled the Hawaiian Islands at least a millennium ago — eyeballing stars from their double-hulled canoes for 2,600 miles. The missionary Hiram Bingham dismissed the Polynesians' sailing expertise, writing off the migration to Hawaii as dumb luck, supposing that they arrived "without much knowledge of navigation" just as "trees from foreign countries repeatedly land on their shores." The Polynesian Voyaging Society proved him wrong in 1976, when Hawaiians sailed a replica of an ancient voyaging canoe to Tahiti in thirty-three days without using navigational instruments.

Anyway, La Pérouse. I was reading about his landing in *Mowee,* Cummins Speakman's history of the island. The inhabitants of Maui charmed the admiral, who found them "so mild and attentive." At the same time, the expedition's physician examined the natives for the not so mild symptoms of venereal disease, debating in his report whether or not this was the legacy of earlier encounters between islanders and Captain Cook's sailors. Typical — the only thing more European than spreading VD is documenting it.

In describing the expedition's scientists' careful record-keeping Speakman notes, "They had been brought up in the encyclopedic atmosphere of the French Enlightenment and their orders contained instructions to observe, measure, and describe everything of interest which they might find in their travels."

I have an undergraduate degree in French language and literature. Affection for the French Enlightenment kind of comes with the diploma, along with a map of the Paris subway and a foolproof recipe for Proust's madeleines. One of my first homework assignments at college was to read Voltaire's *Candide.* I loved the book, but I especially loved discussing the book in class. I had spent my high school years trying to hide just how pretentious I was. So imagine my teenage glee at sitting in a fluorescent-lit room arguing about what Voltaire meant by "we must cultivate our garden." It occurs to me now that the novel is actually about an optimistic young person's disillusionment, but that irony was lost on me.

In another course on French history I fell in love with the *Encyclopédie* Speakman alluded to when he said La Pérouse and his shipmates had come of age in an "encyclopedic atmosphere." Voltaire, Diderot, Rousseau, Montesquieu, and others published their exhaustive compendium of knowledge between 1751 and '72. In more than 70,000 articles, the best French minds explained and classified information on everything from adultery, wild mint, typesetting, and friendship to opera, purgatory, hydraulics, and raccoons. Also, werewolves. (Imagine all the entries on Wikipedia being written by Steve Jobs, Doris Lessing, Garry Wills, Jay-Z, and what's-his-name, that string-theory guy.)

The entire laborious enterprise of the *Encyclopédie* was illumined by curiosity. Thinking about it again was a sort of homecoming for me, a return to my freshman goose bumps over *Candide.* I tracked down Denis Diderot's mission statement for the encyclopedia and wrote it on a purple index card I tacked up next to my desk as a talisman: "All things must be examined, debated, investigated without exception and without regard for anyone's feelings."

Hawaiians, I discovered, take a different approach to collecting, discussing, and presenting information. One afternoon I was sitting at my desk in New York, noodling around the Internet, trying to nail down the meaning of the Hawaiian word *kupuna.* I was reading a message board in which Hawaiians debated whether it simply means any ancestor, starting with one's grandparents, or if it's more specific, for example, a forebear with wisdom or skills to pass on. One quibbler noted, "a *kupuna* needs to be brought up in the tradition." Someone named Hoopii chimed in that a *kupuna* doesn't have to be a blood relative, that the word also has the connotation "to take a person as a grandparent . . . because of affection."

That was an interesting enough notion on its own, but I was intrigued by Hoopii's preface to his opinion. He wrote, "As I read the comments posted by each individual about this specific forum, I do so in respect to each and every single person's beliefs. I sense the passion in each of your concerns and I hope that I do not offend in any way."

Hawaii really is a foreign country, I

thought, turning my head away from the kindly expression of the aloha spirit on my computer screen to look at that Diderot quote tacked to the wall about how entries in the French encyclopedia would be published "without regard for anyone's feelings."

By "anyone" Diderot was taking a jab at the Catholic Church. Incidentally, the Church did have feelings about the *Encyclopédie,* the sort of feelings that got Diderot locked up under house arrest. But Diderot's "anyone" extended beyond the pope to all men of faith, men like Pope Timothy of Yale.

It is worth pointing out that disregard for the feelings of others who disagree is the one thing shared by New England theologians and French philosophers (along with New Bedford whalers, Hawaii-born queen-usurpers, President McKinley, and New York writers finding inspiration in quotations about how it's fine to be a jackass as long as you're trying to tell the truth). In America, on the ordinate plane of faith versus reason, the *x* axis of faith intersects with the *y* axis of reason at the zero point of "I don't give a damn what you think."

"Haole" is a handy little word. And some Hawaiians believe it is a sort of antonym of "aloha," the most Hawaiian word of all.

"Haole" is an old word predating Western contact and can be used to describe nonnative plants and animals as well as people. Still, there's a popular myth that the derivation of the term comes from the phrase for "without breath," *ha* being the word for breath. (As in "aloha," which can be used as a greeting or a farewell or to indicate love but literally means "the presence of breath" or "the breath of life.") This "without breath" interpretation of the word "haole" was supposedly applied to Western visitors because they refused to engage in the traditional Polynesian greeting in which two people touch noses and embrace while breathing each other in.

This blunt assessment suggests that white people are too uptight and alienated from the element of air — from life itself — to perform this fundamental ritual of love and respect. In my case, this judgment is not entirely unwarranted. When Hawaiian hospitality has cornered me into one of these awkward nose-touching, acquaintance-sniffing situations, I have two moves: head-butt the other person, and then wheeze inward as though I were about to dive into a river to pull a baby out of a car that went off a bridge.

■ ■ ■ ■

Not long after Henry Obookiah arrived in New Haven in 1809, Timothy Dwight invited him to live in his home so cousin Edwin could tutor the Hawaiian in English and Christianity. Learning the errors of polytheism and its graven images, Obookiah resolved to return to Hawaii someday and take down the wooden idols of his uncle's profession and "put 'em in a fire, burn 'em up."

At Yale, Henry also met Samuel John Mills, Jr. Mills had been one of the Williams College students in on the "Haystack Meeting" in Massachusetts three years earlier. What happened was, one afternoon in 1806 Mills and his college buddies were out for a walk. Getting caught in a storm, they sought shelter under (or maybe next to) a stack of hay. During this impromptu huddle they got to talking about what red-blooded American boys always discuss while shooting the breeze on a rainy day — how missionaries should be sent to Asia. This brainstorm inspired the formation of the American Board of Commissioners for Foreign Missions, the group that would eventually sponsor the missionaries to the

Sandwich Islands.

Mills brought Obookiah to his father's Connecticut farm and then took him along to Andover Theological Seminary outside of Boston, an institution of such pious gloom townspeople called it "Brimstone Hill."

According to Rufus Anderson of the AB-CFM, Mills had designs on Henry from the get-go, writing a letter after they met at Yale "proposing that Obookiah be sent back to reclaim his own countrymen, and that a Christian mission accompany him."

Mills, Dwight, and the other men of faith who founded the ABCFM would use the empirical data and maps of European explorers like Cook and La Pérouse to fan out evangelists across the Pacific to spread the fear of God as far and wide as Cook's men had spread the clap.

At one of the ABCFM's meetings in Boston in 1813, Dwight began his sermon to the group by quoting Jesus according to John 10:16: "And other sheep I have, which are not of this fold. Them also I must bring, and they shall hear my voice, and there shall be one fold, and one shepherd."

Meanwhile, New England's commercial ships began returning from China with more boys of Obookiah's ilk they'd picked up along the way. In 1816, godly high-rollers in the ABCFM, including Timothy Dwight and his protégé, the Reverend Lyman Beecher, met at New Haven to plan a school for "heathen youths" to be built in Cornwall, Connecticut, a tiny hamlet in the rural Litchfield Hills.

Rufus Anderson of the ABCFM recalled that the founders chose this nowheresville, rather than a city like Boston or New Haven, so as to hinder the foreign students from "acquiring the tastes and habits of city life." Cornwall was not then, nor is it now, known for its theaters. I passed through it a couple of centuries after the school was built, and from what I could tell the closest thing to entertainment was the town blood drive.

The Foreign Mission School opened in 1817, with Edwin Dwight as principal. Its stated task:

> The education, in our own country, of heathen youths, in such manner as . . . will qualify them to become useful missionaries, physicians, surgeons, schoolmasters, or interpreters; and to communicate to the heathen nations such knowledge in agriculture and the arts as may prove the means of promoting Christianity and civilization.

Of the twelve students in the school's first class, seven were from the Sandwich Islands, including Obookiah, Thomas Hopu (Henry's shipmate from the voyage to New York), and a young Hawaiian veteran of the War of 1812 who turned out to be the long-lost son of the high chief of Kauai. The latter was known by various names, including George Sandwich, George Prince, and George Tamoree. Other pupils included an American Indian and two students from the Indian subcontinent.

A report to the ABCFM about the school boasts that the Hawaiians "have renounced their heathenism . . . and testify a deep concern for their idolatrous parents, and brethren, and people." Thankful that "the hand of God" has brought "these lately pagan youths to our shores," the author of this testimony concludes that molding them to return home with the Gospel "may lead to very important events."

Obookiah was the star pupil from the start. By the time he arrived at the school, he had already spent eight years among the seminarians and their families. He had enough English and theology under his belt to start sermonizing to random farmers he bumped into in the woods. In his diary he recounts a walk through the Connecticut countryside when he "found an old grey-headed man, next to the road, hoeing corn . . . and I thought it was my duty to converse with him." To Obookiah, conversing meant informing the man point-blank, "No doubt your days will soon be over." I wonder if the apostle Paul took this approach with the retirees of Corinth. Henry hounded the elderly farmer around his cornfield, haranguing him that anyone that decrepit should repent his sins at once. The codger must not have wanted to waste his dwindling moments on earth being hassled by some prim Polynesian because he ignored Obookiah and "kept hoeing his corn." It's indicative of just how deeply Henry had drunk the Jesus juice that his quintessentially Christian response to this evangelical flop was to offer "thanks to the Almighty God for the opportunity" to pester a geezer with a hoe.

At the Foreign Mission School, Henry studied Euclid, Latin, and Hebrew. He reportedly figured out how to translate Genesis into the Hawaiian tongue years before anyone solved the logistics of Hawaiian spelling and grammar. Working toward becoming "a missionary to my poor countrymen," he paid particular attention to the preaching he heard, finding some of the sermons in Connecticut needlessly baffling to the congregations because of the learned ministers' esoteric vocabulary. After all, "people can't carry [a] dictionary to meeting," he said.

Henry's line of reasoning echoes what Jonathan Edwards meant when he nailed the New England clergy's weakness for the didactic: "Our people do not so much need to have their heads stored as to have their hearts touched." Edwards did so by conjuring images of hearts being shot with God's arrows drunk on sinners' blood. Henry simply decided that when he became a missionary, he would "preach so that all can understand."

Then Henry came down with typhoid fever and died.

He took ill in January of 1818, just months after the school opened. Bedridden for weeks before his death, he confided in one of the Hawaiian students, "It is a good thing to be sick, Sandwich — we all must die — and 'tis no matter where we are." Confident in his salvation, he was not afraid. Still, he did lament, "Oh! How I want to see Hawaii! But I think I never shall. God will do right. He knows what is best."

On February 17, 1818, his friends gathered around his bed and before he died he told them, "Aloha 'oe — my love be with you."

"We thought surely this is he who shall comfort Owhyee," the Reverend Lyman Beecher bemoaned in his funeral sermon for Henry. "We bury with his dust in the grave all our high raised hopes of his future activity in the cause of Christ."

His tombstone in the Cornwall Cemetery is inscribed:

In Memory of Henry Obookiah a native of Owhyee. His arrival in this country gave rise to the Foreign mission school, of which he was a worthy member. He was once an Idolater, and was designed for a Pagan Priest; but by the grace of God and by the prayers and instructions of pious friends, he became a Christian. He was eminent for piety and mission-ary Zeal. When almost prepared to return to his native Isle to preach the Gospel, God took to himself. In his last sickness, he wept and prayed for Owhyee, but was submissive. He died without fear with a heavenly smile on his countenance and glory in his soul. Feb. 17, 1818; aged 26

In 1993, relatives of Henry Obookiah had

his remains reburied at Napoʻopoʻo in Kealakekua Bay, down the road from the remains of his uncle's temple. It's hard to beat the view from his new resting place. But the Litchfield Hills have their charms, especially in the spring, when the countryside is all lilting greenery with the occasional jonquil in bloom.

One April, I had to do a reading in Western Massachusetts so on the way I stopped in Cornwall to see Obookiah's original tomb. There in the village cemetery among the monuments for Yankees with names like Martha, Harriet, and Luther, Obookiah's weathered marker still stands on a gentle slope near the road. The inscription is hard to make out. The centuries have blackened the lettering and the surface of the stone is covered in little trinkets and offerings — corroding coins, strings of shells, a broken coffee mug from Kamehameha Middle School in Kapalama. I'm guessing the Kamehameha mug from Oahu is probably just a memento left there by a well-meaning Hawaiian sixth-grader unaware that Obookiah came to New England in the first place because some of Kamehameha's soldiers stabbed his mom and dad.

The building that housed the Foreign Mission School is long gone, but in front of the Lutheran church that's there now a little plaque is fixed to a boulder. It brags that between 1817 and 1826 it "trained young men of many races to act as Christian missionaries among their peoples."

Henry Obookiah wasn't my only reason for detouring here. Cornwall has ties to an episode from my own Cherokee family's history. Among the hundred or so students from Asia, Greece, and Polynesia who studied at Cornwall, American Indian boys were sent there from southeastern tribes such as the Choctaw and the Cherokee.

I spent weeks on end camped out in archives in Honolulu. And though I'm never more at home than when I'm looking stuff up, I was often envious of locals, the men and women who would come to the Hawaii State Archives to locate an ancestor's grave, the missionary descendants hanging around the Mission Houses Museum archives, poring over the paper trail their forebears left behind. So while paging through one of the page-turners the ABCFM published — compilations of reports from its missions around the globe in places that used to be called Palestine and Ceylon — it was stirring to come across a name I've been hearing my entire life: Elias Boudinot, a Cherokee teenager who, the ABCFM reports, renamed himself after a New Jersey congressman who has "the welfare of our Indians at heart."

Born with the name Buck Watie, Elias Boudinot arrived at the Cornwall school a few months after Obookiah's death. Boudinot and his fellow student and cousin, John Ridge, were caught between the opposing worlds of white and Indian society. They managed to get themselves burned in effigy in Connecticut and then assassinated in Indian Territory by fellow Cherokees.

In attending to the spiritual starvation of Asians and Polynesians, the ABCFM did not neglect the savages here at home. In 1816, the board asked for and received funding from President Madison's secretary of war (who had the purview of Indian affairs) to build a mission house and a school in the Cherokee Nation in Tennessee. The goal there, according to one of the ABCFM annual reports, was "gradually, with divine blessing to make the whole tribe English in their habits, and Christian in their religion."

After the Foreign Mission School was founded in Cornwall, the tribe picked a few boys from among its most prominent families and sent them north. On the way to Connecticut, after visiting former president

Jefferson at Monticello and current president Monroe in Washington, Buck Watie spent a night in Burlington, New Jersey, at the home of a member of the board, Congressman Elias Boudinot. Boudinot was so taken with the boy he offered him a scholarship, and in return Watie took the old man's name, enrolling at the Cornwall school as Elias Boudinot, a name he would hang on to the rest of his life.

Boudinot and Ridge were the school's new Obookiahs. The administration trotted them out before the town, had them write sugary thank-you notes to whites who donated money to the school. But, like Obookiah, John Ridge got sick. Then he fell in love with the teenage daughter of the Cornwall family who nursed him back to health, Sarah Northup. Then he married her. Cornwall, heretofore proud of the school's multicultural mandate, drew the line at miscegenation. A newspaper attacked the marriage as the devious product of "missionary machinery," proposing that the Indian should be "hung" and the "girl ought to be publicly whipped." Then, just as the school was trying to smooth things over with the town, Elias Boudinot proposed marriage to another local white girl, Harriet Gold. Cornwall was once again on fire; this time townspeople burned effigies of Harriet and Elias, with Harriet's own brother lighting the match. Saddened, the secretary of the ABCFM asked, "Can it be pretended, at this age of the world that a small variance of complexion is to present an insuperable barrier to matrimonial connexions?" *Hell, yes!* was Cornwall's answer. The school, already becoming obsolete since the missions abroad were in full swing, couldn't survive another scandal. It shut its doors that year, 1826.

Boudinot and Ridge returned home to the Cherokee Nation with their fair-skinned brides. Boudinot founded and edited the *Cherokee Phoenix,* the tribe's bilingual English/Cherokee newspaper. He collaborated on a translation of the Bible into Cherokee with the ABCFM's missionary, Samuel Worcester. The ABCFM leadership in general, and Worcester in particular, were vocal in support of the Cherokees' struggle to fend off the intentions of the federal government, egged on by the state of Georgia, to remove the tribe from their land. ABCFM secretary Jeremiah Evarts made numerous trips to lobby for the tribe in Washington, D.C., and Worcester lent his name to the landmark Supreme Court decision *Worcester v. Georgia.* This ruling of the

Marshall Court confirmed that the state of Georgia had no jurisdiction over the tribe, an independent nation within the borders of the United States. Too bad the administration of Andrew Jackson refused to execute the ruling and started drawing up plans to evict the tribe across the Mississippi.

John Ridge, Elias Boudinot, Boudinot's brother Stand Watie, along with a hundred or so other Cherokee, saw the inevitability of removal to the West and decided the tribe should at least be paid for their homeland. This cabal met in secret and, with no authority whatsoever, signed the Treaty of New Echota, authorizing the United States to move the tribe in exchange for $5 million and land in what is now Oklahoma. The rest of the tribe protested, sending to Washington a petition signed by nearly all sixteen thousand members of the tribe denouncing the treaty as illegal, but to no avail.

In 1838, the U.S. Army ejected the Cherokee from their homes and rounded them up. One of the places where soldiers gathered the detainees was Ross's Landing on the Tennessee River, site of that first AB-CFM mission the federal government paid for back in 1816. The army marched them across the country at gunpoint in what came

66

to be known as the Trail of Tears, a quarter of the tribe dying along the way.

Standing in that churchyard in Cornwall, looking at the boulder with the little plaque about the Foreign Mission School where Boudinot and Ridge were students, reminded me of when I went to the old Cherokee capital in Georgia and stood on the site of Boudinot's house, where he and his coconspirators signed the Treaty of New Echota. I think I understand Boudinot's motives a little better now. Who would be more inclined to cut his tribe's losses and try and put the Mississippi River between himself and whites than a man who had been burned in effigy by Christian townspeople?

According to a statute passed by the Cherokee Council, signing away tribal land without authorization was literally a crime, punishable by death. Once the tribe got settled in the West, Boudinot and Ridge were executed. Harriet Gold Boudinot had already died from childbirth complications back in Georgia, so she didn't see her husband jumped in the woods and stabbed in the back. But Cornwall's Sarah Northup Ridge watched assassins drag John from their bed in the middle of the night. She witnessed each attacker stab her husband in their yard repeatedly. Then they all took turns trampling his corpse.

Somehow Stand Watie, Boudinot's brother and fellow signer of the Treaty of New Echota, was not put to death. He went on to serve as a general in the Confederate Army in the Civil War. Watie was my great-great-grandfather's commanding officer in the First Cherokee Mounted Rifles. His daughter, my great-grandmother Lena, attended the Cherokee Female Seminary. I have her diploma hanging above my desk. It's dated July 1898, the month President McKinley signed the bill annexing Hawaii to the United States. The founders of the ABCFM would have frowned upon their missionaries' offspring meddling in earthly political affairs in the Pacific, but there's no doubt that Samuel Mills and Timothy Dwight would have been proud that yet another Indian kid graduated Bible school. *And there shall be one fold.*

When Henry Obookiah died in 1818, the stonemason in Cornwall was probably still chiseling that longwinded remembrance on his tombstone the day Edwin Dwight began compiling Obookiah's diary, letters, interviews, and his acquaintances' recollections. *Memoirs of Henry Obookiah* was published in New Haven mere months after the deceased wished his friends a final aloha.

Henry's death was to the Sandwich Islands mission what JFK's assassination was to the Civil Rights Act of 1964. The ABCFM sent to churches a "special call . . . for immediate and liberal help," dropping Obookiah's name to solicit donations for this urgent but costly Pacific venture in light of the heavy burden of the board's responsibilities among the Cherokee. "God loveth a cheerful giver," they said.

The *Memoirs* became a minor bestseller among a certain type of northeastern killjoy. Divinity student Hiram Bingham read the book and made a pilgrimage to Cornwall, recalling, "There were consolations in the reflection that the dear youth had himself been plucked as a brand from the burning, and made a trophy of redeeming mercy." Bingham added that Henry's piety "would fan the missionary spirit and hasten the promulgation of the Gospel on the shores that gave him birth." Bingham was soon spearheading the project. His future shipmate Lucy Thurston described the mission as "the noble enterprise of carrying the light to the poor benighted countrymen of Obookiah." New York farmer Daniel Chamberlain happened upon the book and was so moved he sold his farm, donated the proceeds to the ABCFM, and packed up his wife and five children to set sail for Hawaii on a ship even people without five kids found claustrophobic.

At least Chamberlain had a wife. That was a deal-breaker for the ABCFM. At the last minute, the board decided that the mission's six bachelors — ministers Bingham and Asa Thurston and their four assistants — should marry helpmates but quick. Stars of reality-TV matchmaking shows have known their betrotheds longer than the missionaries knew their wives before shoving off. Luckily, this frantic bride hunt scared up ladies so suited for the task it was like something out of a fairy tale, albeit a fairy tale in which happily ever after involves the married women doing more backbreaking chores than Cinderella suffered before she met her prince. "Each day has been filled up with *hard work,*" is how Mrs. Bingham will describe life in Honolulu.

Friends recommended a schoolteacher named Sybil Moseley to Hiram Bingham and "after I measured the lines of her face . . . with more than an artist's carefulness," he asked an ABCFM elder to arrange a meeting. Their wedding is what normal people refer to as a third date.

Like Obookiah, Sybil had lost both parents. "Alas where will the wide world afford a home for an orphan girl?" she had asked her diary in a youthful fit of despair, not suspecting that the answer would turn out to be the kingdom of the Kamehameha dynasty.

Among her papers, I found a copy of a speech Sybil gave to her female students five years before her marriage. She cautions the girls to avoid reading books "that will injure you, such as novels and the lighter kinds of poetry" and to never go a day without cracking open a Bible. "Cautioning [them] against pride," she advises them to "dress with plainness, neatness, and modesty." She adds, "Often when decorating our vile bodies, let us think, that ere long they will need nothing but a winding sheet, and shroud." The whole lecture reads like a job application to be a preacher's wife.

Lucy Goodale, a Massachusetts schoolteacher, writes her sister in September 1819 that their cousin popped round and talked her into marrying some friend of his and moving to Hawaii. I can just imagine getting a letter like this from my sister: *You mean that place where Captain Cook got killed?* "The gentleman proposed as the companion of my life is Mr. Thurston," she writes.

Sybil Moseley, a motherless schoolmarm yearning to dress plain, has little to lose by throwing in her lot with pedantic adventurers hitting the high seas. Lucy Goodale, however, is a well-educated girl with a large and affectionate family. She's a catch and she is loved. In her memoir, *The Life and Times of Mrs. Lucy G. Thurston,* she writes of going to her father's house and talking through her dilemma with her parents, her uncle, her two brothers and their wives. They agree it's her decision, which almost makes it worse — any family circa 1819 that trusts the judgment of a girl keen to join some Polynesian peace corps is probably worth sticking around.

Asa Thurston is invited to Lucy's parents' house to endure the scrutiny of her relatives and six of her friends. Amid the "free family sociality," they all link arms and engage in an actual sing-along. She recalls that, "introduced at sunset as strangers," she and Thurston would "separate at midnight as interested friends."

That Lucy would willingly exile herself from so much warmth and comfort says something about the depth of her ideals and her steely resolve to live them out. She writes that her friends and country are "dear to my heart" but life is fleeting and "the poor heathen are perishing" without salvation. "Who will give them the Bible, and tell them of a Savior?"

Might as well be her. A month later she left. Afterward, her sister Persis wrote a letter to the sisters-in-law, admitting "it requires all my philosophy, and all my piety" to make peace with the fact that "Lucy is gone, and I can see her face no more."

To a godless heathen like me, there's not much difference between Jehovah and Ku (except that once a year the Hawaiian god of war actually takes time off). But I can't deny the guts of Lucy Thurston and the other brides. Nor do I question their good intentions. Sure, all missions are inherently patronizing to the host culture. That's what a mission is — a bunch of strangers showing up somewhere uninvited to inform the locals they are wrong. But it's worth remembering that these women, and the men they married so recklessly, believed they were risking their own lives to spare strangers on the other side of the world from an eternity in hell.

It took extra courage for the women to sign up for the Hawaiian mission. Aside from the universal trepidation of a long sea voyage and the prospect of adjusting to life in a foreign land, the wives had reasonable concerns about living under what Lucy Thurston feared would be "the iron law of kapus requiring men and women to eat separately." She worried that "To break that law was death. It was death for woman to eat of various kinds of food, such as pork, bananas, cocoa-nuts, etc."

The eating kapus were part of a larger religious, ethical, and legal system, the underlying order for the Hawaiian way of life. Still, who can fault the women for ignoring, say, the ecological ingenuity of the kapu system's land management and obsessing about the severe punishment for certain snacks instead? They had heard tell of Obookiah's aunt being thrown from a cliff for some ethical breach. What if making an innocent faux pas signed a lady's death warrant? Plus, it's hard enough to leave behind one's friends, family, and country; a woman is supposed to give up bacon too?

Recent seminary graduates Hiram Bingham and Asa Thurston were ordained in a Connecticut church a few weeks before shoving off. Reverend Heman Humphrey delivered a sermon in honor of the occasion entitled "The Promised Land," a veritable synopsis of the mind-set of the missionaries and their elders. Humphrey cited Joshua 13:1, "And there remaineth yet much land to be possessed." The world, he argued, "belongs to Christ."

I spent enough time in churches when I was young to know that this has been standard Christian rhetoric for two thousand years. So routine that a reader who goes to Sunday school might just breeze past all the "subduing" and the "belongs" and the "possession" without even noticing it, not questioning the notion that Jesus holds title to the planet. But I can no longer read any faith's Napoleonic saber rattling without picturing smoking rubble on cable news. I guess if I had to pick a spiritual figurehead to possess the deed to the entirety of Earth, I'd go with Buddha, but only because he wouldn't want it.

Reverend Humphrey said, "How large a part of the land of promise remains yet to be possessed." Not that there wasn't still plenty of subduing to do here in North America. "Even within our own limits, the savage still lights his death fires, to appease the wrath of an idol," he points out. What's worse, to the "north, there is an immense region of palpable darkness." (Hi, Canada!)

Thurston and Bingham should have been chastened by this subtext. If New England

Protestants could not even talk Catholic Montreal out of siding with the Antichrist (which is how they see the pope), what makes them think they can douse Hawaii's "death fires" lit for Lono and Ku? After all, Humphrey pointed out, "Satan will not yield the empire of the Sandwich Islands without a struggle."

Lest they forget, the first man who left home to talk up the importance of Jesus — that would be Jesus himself — faced a bit of an uphill climb, an uphill climb in which his executioners forced him to carry the cross they planned to nail him to. "How was the Gospel first propagated, even in an age of miracles?" Humphrey asked. "By toil, by perseverance, by encountering a thousand dangers." As send-offs go, Humphrey's unsettling pep talk reminds me of how my nephew Owen says goodbye on the phone: "I love you! Don't die!"

The missionaries to the Sandwich Islands received the following official instructions from their keepers at the ABCFM: They were supposed to learn to speak Hawaiian and make the natives "acquainted with letters; to give them the Bible with skill to read it." In order to do that, they would need to teach the natives to read, as well as to translate the Bible into Hawaiian. Since it wasn't a written language, they would need to invent a spelling and grammar for it. One person could spend an entire career attempting any one of those things but the board had more job requirements: "You are to aim at nothing short of covering those islands with fruitful fields and pleasant dwellings, and schools and churches; of raising up the whole people to an elevated state of Christian civilization." Is that all?

No. As if the missionaries don't have enough to worry about, the board gives them the seemingly contradictory instruction to not make waves:

> You will withhold yourselves entirely from all interference, and intermeddling with the political affairs and party concerns of the nation or people among whom you reside: paying proper respect to the powers that be, and rendering . . . tribute where tribute is due . . . and showing unto all men a bright and impressive example of a meek and quiet spirit.

In summary, the missionaries' brief was to remake Hawaiian society without aggravating the keepers of the status quo — to butter up the Hawaiian king while teaching his people that the only true authority is the king of kings. What could possibly go wrong? Still, what comes off as a contradiction might be good old-fashioned, New England–style separation of church and state. Just as in the 1600s the Massachusetts Bay colonists would have rioted if ministers had been made magistrates, the same colonists thought it was appropriate for magistrates to consult the ministers and follow the ministers' advice. Church and state were separate but cozy.

Also, the allusion to rendering to the Caesars of the Pacific the proper deference makes sense in light of the evangelists' conviction that the body politic is literally worldly, a distraction from the goal of shepherding as many people into the body of Christ as possible. The ABCFM's instructions to a later company of missionaries to Hawaii spell out this belief: "You are to abstain from all interference with the local and political interests of the people. The kingdom of Christ is not of this world and it especially behooves a missionary to stand aloof from the private and transient interests of chiefs and rulers."

If there is one thing to understand about the New England missionaries, remember that as their defining belief . . . *the kingdom of Christ is not of this world.* A Christian, as the chaplain in *Moby-Dick* put it, "is only a patriot to heaven." The people they are sailing toward? Polar opposite. As Hawaiian historian Samuel Kamakau would assess the missionaries' reception, "Some people helped with the missionary work, and other people belonged to the perpetuation-of-the-earth side."

When I interviewed the Hawaiian independence activist Kekuni Blaisdell, I asked a question about the overthrow of Queen Liliuokalani in 1893. Believe me, he has plenty of things to say about the subject. Both of his grandmothers lived and worked in the queen's household. He was one of the aforementioned protesters marching on the fiftieth anniversary of statehood, carrying "We Are Not Americans" signs. But he didn't get around to discussing the overthrow for a couple of hours, because he answered my opening 1893 question by recounting the history of Hawaii from the beginning of time — literally.

He told me about the earth mother mating with the sky father. They have a daughter, then the sky father mates with the daughter. "The product of conception is stillborn and buried," Blaisdell says. "Up sprouts the first taro plant."

It is an understatement to call the root vegetable, taro, and its mashed form, poi, the staple of Hawaiian food. It's not simply a local favorite, the equivalent of, say, cheese to the French, or cheesesteaks to Philadelphians. As the nineteenth-century English travel writer Isabella Bird noted after a trip to the islands, "A Hawaiian could not exist without his calabash of poi. The root is an object of the tenderest solicitude, from the day it is planted until the hour it is eaten."

One reason for such reverence is that taro is not simply a plant. To ancient Hawaiians, it was a brother. Blaisdell told me that after the taro plant grew from the stillborn's burial, "the next child is the first kanaka." "Kanaka" means human being. Thus, the taro plant is the "number-one sibling." It is a first sibling's responsibility to take care of its younger brothers and sisters. Blaisdell points out that the root of the word for land, *'aina,* is the word for eat. "We eat the land," he says.

The word for Hawaii's commoner class — the people responsible for growing taro and other food — can be translated as "eyes of the land." Meaning, they are the stewards, keeping watch in a reciprocal family arrangement. The land takes care of them and they take care of the land. I tell Blaisdell I have been to Maui, to the remote, old-fashioned taro farm of one of his fellow activists. When I mentioned that on the day I visited the taro patch the farmer was barefoot in the mud, caring for his plants, Blaisdell's eyes lit up and he cooed, "He's a good man!"

Compare that Hawaiian creation myth to the Judeo-Christian one. The first chapter of Genesis claims, "And God said, Let us make man in our image, after our likeness: and let them have dominion over the fish of the sea, and over the fowl of the air, and over the cattle, and over all the earth, and over every creeping thing that creepeth upon the earth." Humans are not caretakers; they are overseers, dominators of their dominion. This conceit comes with some pretty obvious ecological consequences. Plus, in this beginning, the fruit of the land doesn't always nourish the people. In fact, the fruit of knowledge poisons them with fancy ideas and so they are cast out of a garden bearing a striking resemblance to the island of Kauai. (Though having been to the pleasantly sleepy Kauai, I can see how after a few days of lollygagging amidst the foliage, a woman would bite into just about anything to scare up something to read.)

When Blaisdell was telling me how the

Hawaiian people are so rooted in their homeland that they love a root vegetable as a brother, I remembered the little green leather-bound New Testament I was given as a little girl after I learned how to read. It was no bigger than my tiny hands.

Blaisdell and I were sitting outside in Honolulu. I pointed at the cliffs of Nuuanu, supposing that for his people's culture to exist it requires an entire archipelago of mountains and valleys, beaches and farms, whereas the missionaries' entire world was so portable it could fit in a child's pocket. You have to admit, I told him, missionary culture travels light.

The "little band of pilgrims," as Lucy Thurston dubbed the first company of missionaries, assembled at Boston Harbor on October 23, 1819. After hymns and tears, they boarded the brig *Thaddeus,* a vessel so crappy it made the *Mayflower* look like the *QE2.*

On board: the ordained ministers Bingham and Thurston and their wives; a doctor, Thomas Holman, and his wife; the "assistant" teaching missionaries Samuel Ruggles and Samuel Whitney, and their wives; Elisha Loomis, a printer, and his wife; the farmer Daniel Chamberlain and his wife and five children. Also four native Hawaiians who had attended the Foreign Mission School with Obookiah. Three of them were going to help the missionaries: Henry's old shipmate Thomas Hopu, William Kanui, and John Honolii. George Tamoree/Sandwich/Prince/Kaumualii, the son of the high chief of Kauai, was hitching a ride home after his adventures abroad.

The trip took five months. Lucy Thurston compared the cramped quarters of the *Thaddeus* to a "dungeon." They were all so sick for so long Daniel Chamberlain described the ship as a "hospital," though vomitorium would have been more precise. On the bright side, the cramped quarters offered the newlyweds no small amount of quantity time. By journey's end the brides were much better acquainted with their grooms and more or less pleased with the matches. Sybil Bingham wrote in her diary, thanking God for answering her prayer for filling "the void" with a husband like Hiram, a "treasure rich and undeserved." Having read his insufferable memoir, *A Residence of Twenty-one Years in the Sandwich Islands*, all I can say to that is: I'm happy for her?

Just as each marriage had deepened, after five months of throwing up and tripping over one another, five months of huddling together with only Bingham's sermons for entertainment, these people who never expected to see their own relatives again began to think of — and describe — themselves as a family. "Few in our native land can look around on a more interesting and happy family," wrote Mercy Whitney.

Mercy wrote those words in her journal in February, after the brig rounded Cape Horn. Assessing her new mission kin, she noted, "We feel the cords of love binding our hearts together, and uniting them as the heart of one man."

One hundred and eighty-nine years before these Protestants left Boston, the Protestant founders of Boston were sailing toward it. Before they arrived in 1630, John Winthrop, their governor, preached his famous lay sermon hoping New England would become "as a city upon a hill." He declared to the men and women before him, "All true Christians are of one body in Christ." He cited the apostle Paul's address to the church of Corinth: " 'Ye are the body of Christ and members of its parts.' " Winthrop claimed, "The ligaments of this body which knit together are love." Knowing of the hardships he and his fellow colonists would face in Massachusetts, knowing that half the Plymouth pilgrims that preceded them perished in their settlement's first year, Winthrop proclaims that the only way they will survive in the New World is if they stick together and share every burden and every blessing, as "members of the same body." He pleads, "We must be knit together, in this work, as one man."

Mercy Whitney's echo of Winthrop's sentiment, which was an echo of Paul's belief, is a crucial reminder of one of the finest principles of Christianity in general and New England's Congregational brand of Protestantism in particular. Scrape off every irritating trait that mars Mercy and her shipmates — xenophobia, condescension, spiritual imperialism, and self-righteous disdain — and they have an astonishing aptitude for kinship and public-spirited love.

This community-minded devotion is one of New England's lovelier bequests. I can hear it, for instance, in John Adams's inaugural address, when the Puritan descendant rises above his authoritarian streak to marvel that "there can be no spectacle presented by any nation more pleasing, more noble, majestic, or august" than a government comprised of "citizens selected at regular periods by their neighbors to make and execute laws for the general good." Can any noun have more radical sweetness than the word "neighbors" escaping a frumpy New Englander's lips?

Granted, the considerable downside of that region's neighborly disposition is an ill-mannered contempt for anyone who deviates from New England's austere aesthetic and narrow moral code. But that does not make their capacity for community any less beautiful. Knowing how loving they can be to one another just makes their fear of strangers seem all the more pathetic and small.

On March 30, Thomas Hopu spotted the snowy peak of the Big Island's tallest mountain, Mauna Kea. Bingham marveled at the image of "northern winter" peeking up from the "perpetual summer" of Hawaii. Nowadays, that strange contrast is still a wonder, especially from the windows of a helicopter. A few minutes after flying by that chilly summit you can look straight down at the Kilauea volcano, its oozing red maws resembling the mouths of hell the missionaries came there to warn against.

The *Thaddeus* rounded the lush cliffs of the Big Island's northern shore, and as it veered south along the west coast, Maui came into view in the distance. The captain dispatched a crew member in a boat with a couple of the Hawaiians to ask permission to land.

Three hours later the little party returned with big news from shore: Kamehameha the Great was dead. His son Liholiho was the new king. The kapu system was kaput. The idols of the gods had been burned. The temples had been abandoned. The priests were unemployed.

Before the missionaries left New England, one of the board members of the ABCFM gave them their instructions, proclaiming Hawaii's need to be "renovated." It's a concept dear to New England, calling back to the observation of Jonathan Edwards that America was discovered just before the Protestant Reformation, which was "the first thing that God did towards the glorious renovation of the world." Turns out that as the carpenters on the *Thaddeus* navigated the high seas, the Hawaiians were already taking care of some of the demolition.

This upheaval was shocking but it wasn't exactly a surprise. The end of the old system was a natural side effect of the coming of the foreigners whose ships followed those of Captain Cook. In his history of Hawaii, missionary son William DeWitt Alexander asserted that the tradition's collapse was the effect of "deep-seated and widespread causes which had been at work for more than a quarter of a century." Natives witnessed haole sailors breaking rules willy-nilly. Male and female chiefs dined together without incident on board the strangers' ships. Female chiefs secretly wolfed down pork and bananas when the priests weren't looking, and the earth continued to revolve around the sun.

Two of Kamehameha's widows deserve the credit for nudging his son toward reform. The queen mother, Keopuolani, was the highest-ranking noble in all the land. Far fancier than her deceased husband, she was born to the uppermost caste of chiefs. Her parents had been siblings, and brother-sister marriages were prized for concentrating a clan's spiritual *mana,* or power. Children of such unions were especially revered. Native historian David Malo described the intricacies of this phenomenon:

A suitable partner for a chief of the highest rank was his own sister, begotten by the same father and mother as himself. Such a pairing was called *pi'o* (a bow, a loop, a thing bent on itself); and if the union bore fruit, the child would be a chief of the highest rank . . . so sacred that all who came into his presence must prostrate themselves. He was called divine, *akua*.

So as the product of incest among the upper echelon, Keopuolani was doubly blessed. In fact, her body was kapu: anyone greeting her was supposed to prostrate himself before her, including her husband, the nearly seven-foot-tall conqueror. Any commoner who stepped on her shadow was supposed to be put to death, though the queen always politely pardoned offenders. Kamehameha had many wives and other children, but because of her unsurpassed rank, Keopuolani's sons were the undisputed heirs to the throne.

If Keopuolani was Kamehameha's spouse with the most social standing, Kaahumanu was nevertheless his favorite wife. She had unparalleled political clout. Hiram Bingham described Kaahumanu as "magisterial," remarking on "her suavity and skill for managing the minds of others." An English artist who tried to paint her portrait observed, "It must be known that this Old Dame is the most proud, unbending Lady in the whole island. As the widow of [Kamehameha], she possesses unbounded authority and respect, not any of which she is inclined to lay aside on any occasion whatever." Her husband named her his government's *kuhina-nui,* the second-highest office in the land after that of the king — a sort of prime minister, advisor, vice president, and chief of staff all rolled into one.

Kaahumanu hardly relinquished her power when her stepson took the throne. When the chiefs gathered to acknowledge their new king, Kaahumanu informed Liholiho (now also called Kamehameha II), "Hear me, O Divine one, for I make known to you the will of your father. Behold these chiefs and the men of your father, and these your guns, and this your land, but you and I shall share this realm together."

One of Kaahumanu's first items of business was to get her stepson to do away with the eating kapus. In his early twenties, Liholiho had inherited a recently united Hawaiian kingdom just vacated by the fiercest warrior in memory. His father was Kamehameha the Great, and he was merely Kamehameha II. He must have been skittish about ordering a revolution on the first day of his new job, and so he tabled the idea. It was his aristocratic mother who made the first move.

Keopuolani summoned her younger son, Kauikeaouli, and, in full view of the king, she and the little boy ate together. This was a bold gesture that went against everything Liholiho's father had brought him up to protect — literally. When Kamehameha named him heir to the throne, he put Liholiho in charge of protecting the kapus and the temples. That his own sacred mother committed this sacrilege made it easier for him to follow her lead.

I spent an afternoon moseying around the Judiciary History Center in Honolulu with Keanu Sai, a Hawaiian historian, discussing the islands' legal and political developments. I was telling him how my research into Hawaiian culture had made me more aware of my own biases and prejudices than any project I'd ever worked on. I mentioned how my democratic tendencies make me prone to sneer at aristocracy, and yet because of my feminist tendencies I have a soft spot for the domineering Kaahumanu.

Sai pooh-poohed that notion immediately, pointing toward a picture of Kaahumanu hanging on the museum's wall. "She was an effective premier," he said.

Regarding Kaahumanu and Keopuolani's role in ending the kapu system, Sai noted, "There's no need for feminism. They were in control." He added, "In Hawaii, it's not necessarily your gender, it's your rank."

That is a fundamental point. I read Liliuokalani's memoir, *Hawaii's Story by Hawaii's Queen,* twice, once when I started my research and again toward the end of it. She recounts a trip to England during the reign of her brother King Kalakaua when she accompanied her sister-in-law, Queen Kapiolani, to attend Queen Victoria's Jubilee. En route to England, they traveled by train from San Francisco across the United States and made a stop at Mount Vernon. Liliuokalani describes how moved she and Kapiolani were by the sight of George Washington's tomb, "where lie the mortal remains of that great man who assisted at the birth of the nation which has grown to be so great." She continued, "It seemed to me that we were one in our veneration of the sacred spot and of the first President of his country."

This flummoxed me the first time I read it. The birth of the nation the future queen seemed to be admiring happened because George Washington and his army committed treason against their king.

When I read Liliuokalani's book a second time after a couple of years of hanging around Hawaii, I had a clearer understanding of her admiration for Washington. It might have derived from his status and power, not his valor or his republican point of view. He had held the highest office in the land and as the heir to the Hawaiian throne, she was the second-highest-ranking Hawaiian.

The George Washington passage is even more fascinating, given the fact that Liliuokalani's book was published in 1898 to drum up support against the American annexation of Hawaii after she had been deposed from her throne by men with American parents or grandparents who compared their revolution favorably to Washington's.

The last line of *Hawaii's Story by Hawaii's Queen* is addressed to the American people and their congressmen. "As they deal with me and my people, kindly, generously, and justly, so may the Great Ruler of all nations deal with the grand and glorious nation of the United States of America." It's clever to imply that if the U.S. swallows up her little country, God will smite it. As I reread the last sentence of a book written by a Hawaiian queen who was taught to read and write by American missionaries, her final thought seems emblematic of how the hierarchical Hawaiians adapted to Christianity. Jehovah, "the Great Ruler of all nations," is the highest high chief in the universe.

I told Sai that I thought one unfortunate

consequence of 1893 is that Hawaiian commoners never got a chance to overthrow the monarchy themselves, never got to form their own republic. He laughed.

"No! No way," he said. "Hawaii is a system of hierarchy. Chiefly rank was ingrained in the land." He meant that literally, by the way. He explained, "The management of land and resources was intrinsically tied to rank." He brought up the traditional system of land division, the *ahupua'a*, a wedge of land that stretched from the mountains to the sea, ingeniously offering each group of occupants a slice of the ecosystem, allowing access to upland streams and valleys as well as coastal fishing. Each one was lorded over by a chief, Sai says, "who was responsible for the coastline, who put kapu on certain fish to replenish them, who managed access." Thus the most important duty of each land division's chief is to act as that tract's Environmental Protection Agency, to wield authority to guard against such sins as overfishing, so as to insure the people's survival. That chief received tribute, usually foodstuffs, from the commoner farmers and fishermen in his or her domain, and that chief, in turn, paid tribute to the king, who ultimately owned — a better verb might be "controlled" — all the islands. As the Hawaiian Constitution of 1840 defined the situation under Kamehameha I: "To him belonged all the land from one end of the Islands to the other, though it was not his own private property. It belonged to the chiefs and people in common, of whom Kamehameha I was the head, and had the management of the landed property." Unlike feudal European peasants, Hawaiian commoners were not bound to particular tracts of land, and so it behooved the chiefs and king to treat the commoners well so the land in a chief's domain remained productive.

"If it went to a republic," Sai asks, "how would that work? Because then everybody's equal under the same system because they're all citizens."

"I like that," I said.

"Because you're an American," he said. "You should."

Because I am an American, and an argumentative one, I would like to point out that the Hawaiian chiefs were as vulnerable to the trappings of power as any other ruling class in the history of the world, occasionally privileging material goods over ecological stewardship. The most disturbing example of this is Hawaii's participation in the sandalwood trade circa 1790–1830.

The Hawaiian Islands — especially Kauai — were blessed with bountiful stands of sandalwood trees. Sandalwood was one of the rare import items coveted by the Chinese, those consummate exporters of silk, spices, and tea. And so the Hawaiian chiefs made small fortunes by coercing commoners to stop farming and fishing and instead to harvest and haul the trees to port to sell to Western ships. Working conditions in the rainy mountains were treacherous and living conditions deteriorated due to the resulting food shortages when a chief's taro tenders and fishermen were reassigned to logging. "The plain man," David Malo wrote, "must not complain." He noted, "If the people were slack in doing the chief's work they were expelled from their lands, or even put to death."

In the chiefs' defense, their innate human lust for possessions was egged on and exploited by Western traders who were only beginning to solve the trade imbalance with China by pushing opium on the Chinese. (If the word "haole" can have negative connotations depending on inflection and/or the adjective preceding it, it's downright gracious compared to how the Chinese described foreigners — *fan kuei,* "foreign devils" or "ocean ghosts.") By the 1820s, opium consumption was on the rise, but mostly the Chinese were addicted to sandalwood incense and acquiring exquisite sandalwood boxes, many of them carved from Hawaiian trees.

A missionary on Kauai complained to the secretary of the ABCFM in 1830 about the high chiefs' shopping habits, noting, "Some of the foreigners who trade here, are too well acquainted with this trait in their character . . . [and] they urge upon them things which they do not want; and for which, they have no means of paying, but by imposing new burdens upon the people."

Eventually life in areas with concentrations of sandalwood returned to normal, but only because of deforestation. The chiefs didn't stop ordering the commoners to cut down all the sandalwood trees until all the sandalwood trees had been cut down.

In November of 1819 — six months after his father's death and a month after the missionaries sailed from Boston — King Liholiho hosted a banquet at his court in Kailua. (A little north of the bay where Captain Cook was killed, Kailua is on the Big Island's western side, called the Kona Coast.) When the guests arrived for dinner, the women took their seats at the women's table and the men sat at the men's table, per usual. As Kaahumanu later recalled, "Suddenly and without any previous warning [the king] seated himself in a vacant chair at the women's table, and began to eat voraciously." The guests "clapped their hands, and cried out . . . 'the eating taboo is broken.' " Then the king issued orders he wanted carried out on all the islands: the idols were to be burned and the temples were to be abandoned or knocked down.

As a female carnivore, I'm delighted that half the population was freed to eat pork. As a former Smithsonian intern, I am horrified that priceless cultural artifacts went up in smoke. (Many of them were spared, luckily, when believers hid them or buried them in caves, or just generally hung on to carvings for old times' sake.) As the future king David Kalakaua would describe the effects of Liholiho's decree:

In the smoke of burning heiaus, images and other sacred property, beginning on Hawaii and ending at Niihau, suddenly passed away a religious system which for fifteen hundred years or more had shaped the faith, commanded the respect and received the profoundest reverence of the Hawaiian people.

The missionaries interpreted this news as a housewarming gift from God. Lucy Thurston also saw it as fulfilling Henry Obookiah's ambition to return home and gather up idols and "put 'em in a fire, burn 'em up."

She wrote, "Obookiah from on high saw that day. He saw the darkness fleeing away from Hawaii, and that that mission family, so hastily fitted out, was going forth to carry the Bible to a nation without a God."

While relishing the burning of the idols as "the hand of God," Hiram Bingham saw no reason to get overly optimistic about the heart of man.

He concluded that idols being used for kindling only meant that "atheism took the throne." He worried that the king had become Voltaire in a loincloth for having "begun an experiment, like what some equally vain philosophers have often desired, and sometimes recommended, to rule a nation without any recognition of religious obligation, or any respect to the religious views of the people to be governed."

Being a stickler for the Ten Commandments, Bingham couldn't help but point out why a law against graven images became necessary in the first place, when the Israelites "were ever ready, we remembered, to relapse into idolatry." Moses couldn't even take a walk in the woods without his friends and family whipping up a golden calf to worship behind his back, and this was after Jehovah had just parted the Red Sea to save their lives. If an Old Testament tribe that had witnessed the Bible's most over-the-top miracle was still praying to sculptures, Bingham grumbled, "How much more did we fear these uninstructed heathen would do so, unless they could be speedily impressed with the claims of Christianity." Otherwise, Hawaii would be "scourged with atheism or anarchy."

On the long, doltish list of Hiram Bingham's fears, anarchy seems to me the most unfounded. For starters, Liholiho had just doubled his kingly power by eliminating his rivals, the priests. In the English language, the colloquialism "big kahuna" comes from the word for the Hawaiian priests. Who was bigger than the biggest kahuna? That would be the king who decided there wouldn't be any kahunas anymore.

Plus, I cannot think of a more reverent people. When Kekuni Blaisdell was walking me through Hawaiian history from the first taro plant to the present, he made a point of talking up the importance to Hawaiians

100

of the belly button and genitalia. He noted that the navel represents "each person's anatomical attachment to his or her mother," and so "each child is taught to respect [it], to make sure it's clean and to reflect on its significance." He said that genitals are revered as the connection to one's descendants. For that reason, there's a specific genre of hula dance honoring royals, the *hula ma'i,* "that praises the genitalia of the person being honored."

I giggled, and he sighed. "Foreigners find this obscene, uncivilized," he said.

Later, I looked up some of these procreative chants. They're wonderfully metaphorical, enumerating the qualities of a particular king's penis, using images such as a "large sewing needle," or a "bald horse." Still, celebrating royalty's needles and horses, while playful on the surface, is deeply serious business, royal procreation being necessary to continue royal lines.

I envy a people who celebrate their leaders' private parts — that they love those leaders so much they want them making newer, younger versions to tell the next generation what to do. In the democratic republic where I live, any politician whose genitals have made the news probably isn't going to see his name on a ballot again.

Anarchy as a movement or a disposition is difficult to cultivate in a society in which each person knows his place, in which there is nothing more important than hierarchy and lineage, where children clean their belly buttons to honor their ancestors, where rulers' sexuality is not only openly discussed, it is celebrated with choreography because procreation is the root of continuity and tradition.

It's tempting to reduce the initial encounters between Hawaiians and missionaries to some sort of clunky prequel to *Footloose*. After all, when Daniel Chamberlain witnessed his first hula, he wrote, "I scarcely ever saw anything look more Satanic." Yet a procreative hula honoring a high chief strikes me as emblematically Hawaiian because it is *conservative.* The cultural collision of the New Englanders and their new neighbors isn't a quarrel between barefoot, freewheeling libertines and starchy, buttoned-up paragons of virtue (though that is how the missionaries see it). To me, it is the story of traditionalists squaring off.

The *Thaddeus* was anchored off the shore of the Big Island village of Kawaihae, and the missionaries were still waiting for permission to go ashore. They had heard the news of the old religion's demise and were antsy to leap into the spiritual void that awaited them on dry land. In the meantime, a few canoes of native rubberneckers rowed out to the ship "to look at the strangers," as Bingham put it. Staring back, he did not like what he saw: "The appearance of destitution, degradation, and barbarism, among the chattering, and almost naked savages, whose heads and feet, and much of their sunburnt swarthy skins, were bare, was appalling."

The items of clothing that rendered the Hawaiians "almost naked" were the *malo* (loincloth) on the men and the *pa'u* (skirt) on the women. Capes were also an option. These garments were fashioned from *tapa* (also called *kapa*), a soft cloth with the consistency of paper pounded from the bark of mulberry and other trees. Exceedingly beautiful, this cloth was often decorated with intricate, geometric designs. The Bishop Museum in Honolulu, for example, owns a pa'u skirt made out of tapa that belonged to King Liholiho's wife, Queen Kamamalu. Its surface is covered in alternating stripes and checks that would have been a big hit in a Bauhaus design studio.

Captain Cook was smitten with this textile when he first saw it in Kauai in 1778. He wrote in his journal, "One would suppose that they had borrowed their patterns from some mercer's shop in which the most elegant productions of China and Europe are collected. . . . The regularity of the figures and stripes is truly surprising."

One of the missionaries who arrived a few years after the Bingham company took the time to observe the time-consuming process by which Hawaiian women pounded the bark and then decorated it. He concluded that its production takes so much "invention and industry" it proves the Hawaiians were not "incapable of receiving the improvements of civilized society." For a missionary, where there's drudgery, there's hope. That epiphany came later, however. The Bingham gang probably dared not look closely enough to appreciate the merits of this native art form; they were likely averting their eyes from bare breasts and thighs.

Lucy Thurston recoiled at the native dress, or lack thereof, remarking, "To a civilized eye their covering seemed to be revoltingly scanty." Still, unlike Bingham, she rallied when some of the visitors handed her a recently allowed banana through her cabin window. She passed back some biscuits in return and they called her "wahine makai" — good woman. She was touched by their hospitality, later recalling, "That interview through the cabin window of the brig *Thaddeus* gave me a strengthening touch in crossing the threshold of the nation."

On April 1, some Hawaiian chiefs boarded the *Thaddeus,* among them the prime minister, Kalanimoku. Bingham lauded him as "distinguished from almost the whole nation, by being decently clad." Lucy Thurston was also impressed, marveling that he had "the dignity of a man of culture." By which she meant he was wearing pants — yellow ones, along with a silk vest and a fur hat. He bowed to the ladies and shook their hands. Years later, Lucy remembered, "The effects of that first warm appreciating clasp, I feel even now."

Two of the female chiefs, widows of Kamehameha, sat politely on chairs for a while, and then sprawled on floor mats, one of them disrobing. "While we were opening wide our eyes," Lucy wrote, "she looked as self-possessed and easy as though sitting in the shades of Eden."

Bingham approached Kalanimoku about establishing the mission, but the minister waved him off and "referred us to the king."

Kalanimoku did escort Bingham and Thurston on shore, taking them sightseeing to the recently abandoned temple of Pu'ukohola at Kawaihae Bay. Devoted to the war god Ku, the site is now administered by the National Park Service. This was the last major temple complex built before the end of the kapu system. This sort of pyramidal lava-rock structure measures 224 by 100 feet, and rises twenty feet high. Perched on a hill overlooking the water, this might be the most awe-inspiring manmade monument in all the islands aside from Ku's new digs, the naval base at Pearl Harbor.

Before Kamehameha's uncle, the high chief, died, he named his nephew the keeper of Ku. Kamehameha had the temple built because of a prophecy promising that if he did, he would conquer all the islands. Thousands of people formed a human chain to pass lava rocks from twenty-five miles away, stacking the stones without any mortar. This is where Kamehameha invited his cousin and rival for a peace conference and then had him killed on arrival and sacrificed to Ku.

In 2008, the *Honolulu Star-Bulletin* ran an article titled "Betrayed Bloodline Looks Past Transgression," about how one of the assassinated cousin's descendants bucked two centuries of family grudge tradition to chair the Kamehameha Day festivities in the city of Hilo. The man admitted that his relatives "still harbor bad feelings toward Kamehameha to this day."

Like so many Hawaiian locations with bloody pasts, Pu'ukohola is absurdly picturesque. The temple is one man's tribute to his violent god, built out of a craven lust for spiritual and political domination and christened with his kinsman's blood. Still, a swell place to spend an afternoon.

Hiram Bingham found Kamehameha's temple "a monument of folly, superstition and madness, which the idolatrous conqueror and his murderous priests had consecrated with human blood to the senseless deities of Pagan Hawaii." He hoped that "soon temples to the living God would take the place of these altars of heathen abomination." To that end, Kalanimoku and the other chiefs sailed south with the missionaries toward the king's court in Kailua.

On board the *Thaddeus,* Bingham preached his first Sunday sermon in Hawaii on "the design of the Messiah to establish his universal reign, and to bring the isles to submit to him." Before this makeshift congregation of natives and New Englanders, Bingham cited Isaiah's prophecy of his god's ambition: "He shall not fail nor be discouraged till he have set judgment in the earth: and the isles shall wait for his law."

A missionary preaching the first sermon in an archipelago pretty much has to quote that verse. Otherwise, it would be like a Bon Jovi concert without "Livin' on a Prayer." Still, I wonder if this sermon was the smartest teaser, Bingham announcing to the locals that he and his friends had come all that way just to introduce harsh new rules and regulations. Why not start with something comforting and poetic, such as the Psalms or more impressive, like one of Jesus' magic tricks — hook them with Christ's ability to raise the dead and walk on water, maybe get around to the fine print about Judgment Day later? Not that Bingham had the natives' undivided attention.

"How unlike to those peaceful Sabbaths I have enjoyed in America, have been the scenes of this day," Nancy Ruggles wrote of that first service. She complained of being "thronged with these degraded natives, whose continual chattering has become wearisome to me." Still, she wasn't bored, admitting, "I think this has been the most interesting Sabbath of my life."

The next day, according to Lucy Thurston, "The first sewing circle was formed, that the sun ever looked down upon in the Hawaiian realm" to make a frock for one of the queens. Or, according to Bingham, the women "fitted out the rude giantess with a white cambric dress." The New Englanders were more than happy to stitch coverings to hide this queen's ample flesh. Looking back on that day, Lucy would brag, "The length of the skirt accorded with Brigham Young's rule to his Mormon damsels, — *have it come down to the tops of the shoes.* But in the queen's case, where the shoes were wanting, the bare feet cropped out very prominently."

After passing Mount Hualalai, an extinct volcano, the ship arrived in Kailua. This court was where Kamehameha died and where his son broke the kapu by eating with women. Nowadays, what had been the royal compound is King Kamehameha's Kona Beach Hotel. In 1820, when the *Thaddeus* anchored there, hundreds of natives, including King Liholiho and his mother, frolicked half-naked in or near the water. Spying them surf, sunbathe, and dance on the beach, Bingham carped that they "exhibit the appalling darkness of the land, which we had come to enlighten."

Bingham, Thurston, and Thomas Hopu went ashore to meet King Liholiho in his thatched house. According to Lucy Thurston, "They found him eating dinner with his five wives" — and she adds that "two of his wives were his sisters, and one the former wife of his father."

The ministers read the king letters from the American Board of Commissioners for Foreign Missions explaining their intentions in his kingdom. "We made him the offer of the Gospel of eternal life," wrote Bingham, "and proposed to teach him and his people the written life-giving Word of the God of Heaven . . . and asked permission to settle in his country, for the purpose of teaching the nation Christianity, literature and the arts."

The king, Bingham griped, "was slow to consent." Liholiho promised to think about it. The missionaries spent the next few days waiting around, pestering him for permission to settle. The only thing worse than a missionary coming to your house is a whole troupe of missionaries coming to your house day after day, begging to move next door. One day they brought the king an extravagant Bible they had intended to give his father. Then they invited him to dinner on the *Thaddeus* and sang him hymns. Another time he made the excuse that he couldn't give them an answer until he consulted Queen Kaahumanu, who was away on a fishing trip. One morning the white men and women paid a visit to the king's house and were scandalized to learn he was still in bed at eleven o'clock. Sybil Bingham wondered if he kept them waiting because of the Hawaiians' "great indolence and total disregard of time."

Another reason the missionaries worried Liholiho was procrastinating about making a decision on whether or not to let them stay was their belief in monogamy. According to Lucy, Thomas Hopu had revealed to the king "that our religion allowed neither polygamy nor incest. So when Kamamalu, his sister and marked favorite out of five queens, urged the king to receive the Mission, he replied: 'If I do they will allow me but one wife, and that will not be you.' " True enough, though if the king read the first half of that Bible of theirs, he could have found a counter-argument or two, what with Moses' mother also being his aunt, or Lot being his grandchildren's father (though, technically, his daughters did get him drunk and rape him).

During one of the missionaries' pleas to start their work, they proposed to Liholiho that some of them could stay in Kailua at his court while others would set up shop in Honolulu, already frequented and prized by Western sailors for its impressive harbor.

Bingham recalled, "To this proposition the king replied, 'White men all prefer Oahu. I think the Americans would like to have that island.' " This offhand remark is so prophetic it is taking all my writerly restraint not to italicize it.

Finally, after two weeks of thumb twiddling, Liholiho granted the missionaries permission to start a mission, but only on a trial basis for one year. Bingham wrote that they promised the king "that we should send for no more missionaries, till our experiment had been made and approved."

There was a reason Liholiho kept putting off authorizing the mission and it had little to do with him being a late sleeper. Nor did the king who had summarily given the ax to all the priests of Hawaii worry that a couple of pencil-necked seminary grads from New England would prevent him from sleeping with any relative he damn well pleased. No, Liholiho's problem was that he was afraid that allowing American settlers in his realm would offend the king of England.

According to the journal of Captain George Vancouver of the Royal Navy, in 1794, Liholiho's father, Kamehameha, made "the most solemn cession possible of the Island of Owhyhee to his Britannic Majesty." Kamehameha and his chiefs, Vancouver wrote, "unanimously acknowledged themselves subject to the British crown." For this the captain gave the king a Union Jack. There is no record that the British government ever acknowledged receipt of the gift of Hawaii. That's how stuck up the British were — whole archipelagoes were handed to them and they were too busy ruining continents to notice. But the Hawaiians didn't know that. Kamehameha I and Kamehameha II believed they ruled a British protectorate. This is the reason that the Hawaiian flag features a Union Jack.

On my stroll through the Judiciary History Center with Keanu Sai, we were discussing how King Liholiho kept the missionaries waiting for days on end to give them an answer about whether or not they had permission to settle in Hawaii. Sai points out that this procrastination goes back to Liholiho's father. "Kamehameha," he said, "was British."

Sai continues, "In 1810, Kamehameha I was sending letters to King George III, advising him of the consolidation of the Sandwich Islands under one rule, that [George] is now king of the Sandwich Islands." Kamehameha reassured the king that "he was his obedient servant."

"It was after that," Sai says, that Kamehameha "began to implement British governance. That's when you start to see the words 'prime minister' being used. And that prime minister was Kalanimoku."

Kalanimoku is the aforementioned gentleman who made such a good first impression on the missionaries for his courtly manner and wearing of pants. "His nickname," Sai says, "was Billy Pitt." William "Billy" Pitt was then the prime minister of Great Britain, whom Sai describes as Kalanimoku's "counterpart."

When Kamehameha ceded the islands to George Vancouver, he also granted the Englishman permission to send missionaries — *British* missionaries. "So when the [American] missionaries showed up in 1820," Keanu Sai said, "the chiefs knew missionaries were coming. The problem they had was they weren't British. That's why they made them sit there off the coast and said, 'You're going to sit there until we find out what we're going to do with you,' because that could affect their allegiance to Great Britain. So John Young" — an Englishman who was a trusted advisor to the Kamehamehas — "was told to go on the ship, find out who they are, why they are here. And then he came back and he said, 'Same religion, different nationality.' "

Regarding the missionaries' temporary permission to evangelize, Sai maintains, "The chiefs were watching them, saying, 'We're going to see how you folks operate.' " The missionaries' one-year probation was renewed four times. It wasn't until four years after the New Englanders' arrival that the government allowed them to settle permanently, a ruling made, according to Sai, "after Liholiho traveled to London to meet with King George." He adds, "Now, that tells me who's in control."

Lucy Thurston wrote, "After various consultations, fourteen days after reaching the Island, April 12th, permission simply for one year, was obtained from the king for all the missionaries to land upon his shores." Lucy and Asa Thurston planned to stay in Kailua, along with Dr. Holman and his wife. ("God will be our physician," groaned Sybil Bingham, who was moving on to Honolulu.) The Kailua settlers were joined by two of the Hawaiians from the Cornwall school, William Kanui and Thomas Hopu. Hopu, Henry Obookiah's old shipmate, was Reverend Thurston's interpreter, translating the missionary's sermons until Thurston could learn the Hawaiian language.

"Such an early separation was unexpected and painful," said Lucy about saying goodbye to her friends from the *Thaddeus*. "At evening twilight we sundered ourselves from close family ties, from the dear old brig, and from civilization."

Before he sailed on to Honolulu, Hiram Bingham escorted the Thurstons and the Holmans to their new home. "A small thatched hut was by the king's order appropriated for their accommodation," he wrote, "if such a frail hut . . . without flooring, ceiling, windows, or furniture, infested with vermin, in the midst of a noisy, filthy, heathen village can be said to be for the *accommodation* of two families just exiled from one of the happiest countries in the world."

Describing their new abode, Lucy wrote, "There was a secret enemy whose name was legion lying in ambush." Satan? "It was the *flea*."

"For three weeks after going ashore," wrote Lucy, "our house was constantly surrounded, and our doors and windows filled with natives. From sunrise to dark there would be thirty or forty at least, sometimes eighty or a hundred." The white women, she noted, were "objects of curiosity." Hawaiians had seen a steady stream of white men since the arrival of Captain Cook forty-two years earlier, but staring at Lucy and the doctor's wife became something of a fad. The Hawaiians followed the ladies around like paparazzi. One day, fed up with being ogled, Lucy left the house to go sit under a tree for a little privacy. "In five minutes I counted seventy companions."

The Thurstons' only chairs were overturned buckets. Not that they had much time for sitting. Living at Liholiho's court, Lucy observed that to the king and the chiefs the "highest point of etiquette . . . was, *not to move,*" but the life of "an American lady, the active wife of a missionary, could not be measured by such a yardstick." Three or four times a day, Liholiho's wives would drop by for lessons or to socialize. Referring to a pair of biblical sisters who befriended Jesus — Mary, who according to the Book of Luke "sat at the Lord's feet and listened to what he was saying," and Martha, the busybody homemaker "distracted by her many tasks" — Lucy wrote, "When the queens were at our house, we sisters were Marys; when they were away, we were Marthas."

One aspect of life at Kailua complicating their many Martha-like chores was the beachfront settlement's distance from inland fresh water sources. Then, as now, the west coast of the Big Island is prized for its beaches and sunny days (as opposed to the east coast around Hilo, which locals call the "rainy side"). Kamehameha I and II would not have been surprised the haoles would someday build their five-star resorts along this stretch of shore between the Pu'ukohola temple and the Kailua court. It is an excellent location for water sports and getting a suntan. Lucy mentions "hundreds of natives, all ages, of both sexes, and every rank, bathing, swimming, floating on surf boards." It is, however, a lame location for doing oodles of laundry by hand. Hawaiians were used to hauling drinking water to the shore. But the cleanliness required by godliness meant that the missionaries required way more water resources than the natives. As Lucy points out, "Every quart of water was brought to us from two to five miles in large gourd shells, on the shoulders of men." The scarcity of water and all-around regret would send the Holmans scurrying back to the mainland after three months.

Hiram Bingham recalled that King Liholiho, "when he learned with what promptness we could teach reading and writing, objected to our teaching the common people these arts before he himself should have acquired them." Bingham finds this attitude "encouraging, for we wished him to take the lead" but also "embarrassing, for we wished to bring the multitude under instruction, without reference to the distinctions of birth or rank."

Within three months, Hiram Bingham reported, the Thurstons, with help from Thomas Hopu, had taught the king to read a little of the New Testament. But according to Lucy, soon thereafter "the pleasures of the cup caused his books to be quite neglected." However, Liholiho's little brother, Kauikeaouli (the boy their mother had defied the kapu laws to eat with), "attended to his lessons regularly." Bingham praised the boy, a "promising pupil" who could "spell English words of four syllables."

"Watchfulness, on our part," Bingham writes, "was demanded not to provoke needless hostility or to wound unduly the self esteem of the grandees, and at the same time not to omit to do good to them and their needy people according to the explicit commands of the Bible."

"Under such a despotic government," Lucy asserted, "it was all important that those in authority be taught and Christianized. It was forging a key that would unlock privileges to a nation." This was both an astute tactic as well as the missionaries' only choice, given the king's initial denial of literacy to commoners. For instance, tutoring the king's younger brother was a wise investment of Lucy Thurston's limited time. The child would eventually succeed his sibling and become King Kamehameha III, the longest-reigning monarch of the Hawaiian Kingdom. Lucy must have swelled with pride a few years later when her former student ascended the throne and outlawed adultery. (That word, by the way, did not exist in the Hawaiian vocabulary and so, technically, the government of Kamehameha III outlawed the delightful crime of "mischievous mating.")

One day, Lucy was in her house, tutoring the prince, when one of the unemployed priests burst in. He was drunk. Before she knew it, her student and his entourage had vanished, leaving her alone in the house with the invader, who "threw himself upon the bed and seemed to enjoy the luxury of rolling from side to side upon its white covering." He then chased her around the house and out into the yard, where Lucy bashed him with a stick and ran away. She sprinted to fetch her husband and they returned home, where she collapsed into "trembling and tears." Soon the house was filled with concerned chiefs. "The queens were very sympathizing," she recalled.

"With tears they often tenderly embraced me, joined noses and said: 'Very great is our love to you.' "

Lucy and Asa's grandson, Lorrin A. Thurston, would go on to be one of the leaders of the coup d'état against the Hawaiian queen in 1893. In his memoirs, he wrote of his grandmother, "She was as much a missionary as her husband." Her work as a teacher, he pointed out, was "not only as a literary teacher, but as a teacher of housekeeping, sewing, cooking, and care of children." For this, he marveled, she "received no salary whatsoever." And not only that, she managed her household on the miserly stipend the American Board of Commissioners for Foreign Missions paid her husband. Lorrin Thurston writes that his grandmother once told him a story "illustrating the economical character of the American Board":

The family was without a dictionary; she proposed to the children that, if they would go without butter made from the milk of the family cow, she would sell the butter and buy a dictionary with the proceeds. The children agreed, and the book was bought, but afterward, the authorities of the American Board having discovered how she obtained it, the cost was deducted from her husband's salary.

Lucy delivered one of those children on a schooner headed toward a missionary meeting on Oahu. Giving birth, from what I've seen on sitcoms, looks painful enough on dry land. Lucy had her baby in the throes of seasickness. Then, later on, after a Honolulu doctor diagnosed her with breast cancer, he deemed chloroform too risky for her mastectomy and so she was wide awake for an hour and a half, sitting up straight in a wooden chair while the doctor sliced off her breast, her blood spattering his eyes.

Her take on the operation was that it "inspired me with freedom." Afterward, she proclaimed, "I am willing to suffer. I am willing to die. I am not afraid of death. I am not afraid of hell."

When the time came to ask the missionary board for new blood, reinforcements to aid the pioneer company in their work, Asa Thurston sent headquarters a description of the qualities to look for in an applicant. His ideal missionary bears a striking resemblance to his wife, the good sport:

We want men and women who have

souls, who are crucified to the world and the world to them, who have their eyes and their hearts fixed on the glory of God in the salvation of the heathen, who will be willing to sacrifice every interest but Christ's, who will cheerfully and constantly labor to promote his cause. . . . The request which we heard while standing on the American shores, from these islands, we reiterate with increasing emphasis: "Brethren, come over and help us."

If I had to pick one Bible verse that students of American history should know, it is Acts 16:9: "And a vision appeared to Paul in the night; There stood a man of Macedonia, and prayed him, saying, Come over into Macedonia and help us." In the middle of his second missionary journey, the apostle Paul had a dream or a hallucination in which a Macedonian stranger pleaded for his preaching. Paul dropped what he was doing in Asia Minor and "immediately" sailed across the Aegean.

Theologians refer to this as the "Macedonian call." For example, in his "Letter from a Birmingham Jail," Martin Luther King, Jr., writes: "Like Paul, I must constantly respond to the Macedonian call for aid."

For Americans, Acts 16:9 is the high-fructose corn syrup of Bible verses — an all-purpose ingredient we'll stir into everything from the ink on the Marshall Plan to canisters of Agent Orange. Our greatest goodness and our worst impulses come out of this missionary zeal, contributing to our overbearing (yet not entirely unwarranted) sense of our country as an inherently helpful force in the world. And, as with the apostle Paul, the notion that strangers want our help is sometimes a delusion.

The forerunners of the New England missionaries, the Massachusetts Bay colonists, invented American exceptionalism, scrawling Acts 16:9 across their colony's official seal, in which an Indian literally says, "Come over and help us." (The natives of Massachusetts didn't have an official slogan but the few who had not been struck dead by smallpox spread by foreigners would have been better served by a more specific slogan along the lines of "Please don't burn our wigwams while our babies sleep inside.")

When Yale's Timothy Dwight delivered the founding sermon at Asa Thurston and Hiram Bingham's alma mater, Andover

Theological Seminary, Dwight praised the doctrines carried to the New World "by those eminently good men, who converted *New-England* from a desert into a garden." Hoping to inspire the Puritans' godly descendants to keep on gardening, Dwight preached that " *'Come over to Macedonia, and help us,'* is audibly resounded from the four ends of the earth. . . . The nations of the East, and *the islands* of the sea, already *wait for his law.*"

Acts 16:9 is the meddler's motto, simultaneously selfless and self-serving, generous but stuck-up. Into every generation of Americans is born a new crop of buttinskys sniffing out the latest Macedonia that may or may not want their help.

For the Thurstons and their brethren, it was Hawaii. Asa and Lucy spent forty years in Kailua. In 1837 their congregation built a church out of lava rocks from old Hawaiian temples. It is still standing, and still a church. A model of the *Thaddeus* is on display in the sanctuary.

As the Thurstons were settling in on the Big Island, Hiram Bingham and the rest of the pioneers on the *Thaddeus* sailed northwest, past Maui, Lanai, and Molokai, toward Oahu. Nearing Honolulu on April 14, 1820, Maria Loomis, the printer's wife, wrote,

"The first object that attracted our attention was a lofty craggy point called Diamond hill."

Even now, spotting Diamond Head from the window of a plane about to land at Honolulu International is still one of Hawaii's most consistent little thrills. The iconic volcanic crater's Hawaiian name, Leahi, means "brow of the tuna" and it does look more animal than mineral. There might be taller or prettier mountains in the islands but I'm hard pressed to think of one that's more magnetic. Like a television, if it's in my field of vision, I cannot pay attention to anything else.

As the brig began to curve around the coast, Maria Loomis continued, "Our eyes were feasted with the verdant hills & fertile vallies." She described groves of coconut palms lining the beaches.

The *Thaddeus* waited in the harbor with the company while Hiram Bingham and a small party rowed ashore to look for the island's high chief. They trudged through the then-dusty plain of Honolulu and climbed Punchbowl Hill, another volcanic crater presiding over what is now downtown. Bingham wrote, "We had a beautiful view of the village and valley of Honolulu, the harbor and ocean, and of the principal mountains of the island."

From there they looked across at Diamond Head and Waikiki, to the fort by the harbor, and at the soupy taro patches in the inland valleys. Bingham, in an uncharacteristic fit of poetry, praised the sight of the staple crop "with its large green leaves, beautifully embossed on the silvery water in which it flourishes."

Bingham compared himself to Moses gazing at the Promised Land. Noticing the cliffs of Nuuanu, the site of "the last victory of Kamehameha," he predicts the landscape "was now to be the scene of a bloodless conquest for Christ."

The Christian soldiers' weaponry, he said, would be "the school, the pulpit, and the press."

Remember the opening credits of *Hawaii Five-O*, when Jack Lord stands on a roof, surveying the panorama of then-mod Honolulu? I'm on a balcony — around here it's called a "lanai" — on the twentieth floor of the very same building, the Ilikai. While I command the same view as Jack and his jawline, this morning it's yet another voggy day. Vog, the volcanic fog blowing over here from Kilauea, is the most exotic air pollution my landlubber's lungs have ever coughed up.

Wish I could say I was taking the Ilikai's elevator down to street level so as to get cracking on a day of thwarting PCP smugglers or rescuing the diabetic scientist kidnapped by my Red Chinese archenemy, like Jack used to do every week. I chose to stay in this building because it's walking distance to the Mission Houses Museum's library and archives in downtown Honolulu, where the closest thing to a felony is taking notes with an ink pen instead of a pencil. Perusing the letters and diaries the New England missionaries left behind is detective work of a sort, albeit an investigation whose only theme song is the faint rhythm of a gloved hand paging through the brittle correspondence of the dead.

When I was browsing through a box of papers belonging to Abner Wilcox, a Connecticut-born proselytizer on the island of Kauai, I found a memo he received in 1838 from the American Board of Commissioners for Foreign Missions asking its missionaries scattered around the globe to send back to Boston items for a cabinet of curiosities they were assembling at headquarters, including "warlike weapons" because "these convey a vivid idea of the savageness of heathenism, and impress the beholder with the reality of the dark places of the earth, which are full of the habitations of cruelty."

Speaking of the habitations of cruelty, the Ilikai was designed by one of the architects of Seattle's Space Needle. It was the very first luxury high-rise hotel in the state. Elvis used to stay here. Its developer, Chinn Ho, was a self-made millionaire who rose from peddling can openers to become the first Asian to run the Honolulu Stock Exchange. Detective Chin Ho Kelly on *Hawaii Five-O* was named after him. Which is a nice change of pace, since most things around here are named for long-dead Hawaiian monarchs. Like, I wonder if Chin Ho Kelly or Chinn Ho himself got their cavities filled at the King Kalakaua Dental Center.

I liked the symmetry of waking up in the islands' first residential high-rise and walking to work at the islands' first wood-frame house. The Mission Houses Museum complex contains the buildings in which Hiram Bingham and his colleagues lived and worked, including a wooden prefab shipped from Massachusetts.

I took a guided tour led by Mike Smola, the museum's affable tour coordinator. After hitting the highlights about the American Board of Commissioners for Foreign

Missions and discussing Henry Obookiah, he says, "During the forty-three years the mission station operated, between 1820 and 1863, they established seventeen stations on five major islands. Twelve separate companies, or groups of missionaries, arrived, all totaling about one hundred and seventy-eight people. But the station here in Honolulu, which was situated on the land you're standing on presently, was the headquarters, or main mission station for the entire endeavor."

A portrait of Hiram and Sybil Bingham hangs on the wall. Smola points out that it was "painted before they left Boston in 1819 by an old buddy of Reverend Bingham's, Samuel F. B. Morse, as in the Morse code and the telegraph."

I love Morse's stirring portrait of the Revolutionary War hero the Marquis de Lafayette hanging in New York's City Hall. Morse was in Washington painting it when he received the news his wife was ailing back home in Connecticut. He raced toward her but by the time he arrived, she had died. And so he started monkeying around with a machine to speed up communication, an achievement that would eclipse the reputation of his art.

Morse was born into a venerable family of

New England Protestants. His minister father, Jedidiah, had founded a newspaper with Timothy Dwight and others to guard "morals, religion and the state of Society in New England." Not only was Jedidiah Morse on the American Board of Commissioners for Foreign Missions, he had been one of the clergymen who lobbied for the founding of the seminary at Andover that Hiram Bingham and Asa Thurston attended.

Hence, the younger Morse's acquaintance with, and portrait of, Bingham, as well as his images of Thomas Hopu and the other three Hawaiian men who would soon sail on the *Thaddeus*. Morse lit the Binghams with a liturgical glow. Hiram smolders with his dark eyes and peacock's plume of hair. Sybil looks clean.

Smola points to a model of the neighborhood as it looked in 1821, the year after the arrival of the missionaries, or "mikanele," as the Hawaiians called them. Nowadays, grassy lawns and fine old trees beautify this area of downtown. The same land in the model is all dirt brown. "The first thing I'd like to point out is how dry this area is," Smola says. "It's practically a desert." Water had to be hauled in from the Nuuanu Stream a couple of miles inland.

Smola indicates four little huts built out of pili grass, the "tufted grass that was the preferred building material of the Hawaiian people." In his memoir Hiram Bingham wrote, "A house thus thatched assumes the appearance of a long hay stack." Fitting that a pious expedition first envisioned at the Haystack Meeting in Massachusetts would find New England missionaries holed up in thatched homes in Polynesia — much to Hiram Bingham's dismay. "Such houses," he grumbled, "are ill adapted to promote health of body, vigor of intellect, neatness of person, food, clothing or lodging, and much less, longevity. They cannot be washed, scoured, polished, or painted." They are no place, he continued, "for the security of valuable writings, books, or treasures." He would be relieved to learn that some day the mission's descendants would build a climate-controlled library next door to care for (and lock up) his and his fellows' writings.

Smola says the missionaries lived in the huts "until the completion of this building here, which is a New England–style wooden frame house. It was something of a prefabricated building. The lumber was cut in New England and then shipped here for the mikanele to assemble, which they had done by the end of 1821. Today it is the oldest still-standing wood-frame structure in all of the Hawaiian Islands."

The house, Smola points out, features "small windows, short ceilings, and no good breezeways. In short, it's built to keep the New England winter out. Of course those are difficult to find here in the tropics."

Eventually, the missionaries learned to position their windows so as to circulate breezes from the trade winds. Still, the buildings they and their progeny constructed in the decades to come replicated this first one. There's barely a back road or highway in Hawaii that doesn't have at least one wee whitewashed house of worship. It can be unsettling to take a thirteen-hour flight from the East Coast to Maui only to turn a corner and stumble upon a scene straight out of Old Saybrook.

On her tour of the islands in 1873, Englishwoman Isabella Bird analyzed the haoles' dwellings. "Some look as if they had been transported from the old-fashioned villages of the Connecticut Valley, with their clap-board fronts painted white." And yet, she noticed, "The New England severity and angularity are toned down and draped out of sight by these festoons of large-leaved, bright-blossomed, tropical climbing plants."

To me, the most evocative example of prim American architecture imposed on the exotic landscape is in Hanalei, on the island of Kauai. This was the town where the 1958 musical *South Pacific* was filmed, its mountains the backdrop for "Bali Hai." Sunsets there are downright lurid.

William Patterson Alexander, a missionary who sailed with the ABCFM's fifth company to Hawaii, erected the Waioli mission house there in 1837. White and wooden, the building is nestled at the foot of Hanalei's undulating peaks, its right angles softened by palm trees in the lush front yard. It's as if Gauguin had plopped one of the French farm maids from his early paintings — wholesome girls in starched caps who look like they make their own cheese — into the vivid sensual scenery of his later Tahitian canvases.

Mike Smola leads the way through the Honolulu mission house's cramped chambers — the communal dining room with its Chinese dishes, the kitchen with its beehive oven. He says, "Mrs. Bingham writes in her journal about baking as many as thirty loaves of bread a day in this oven. Which brings up something of an interesting point about the mikanele diet. They originally came here expecting to keep their New England diet, their beef, dairy, wheat, and potatoes. No way. Even today, living out here like that is an incredibly expensive proposition. So they very quickly adapted to a native diet. They ate fish, poi, local fruits and vegetables, and chickens. Now, they did get food supplies from the ABCFM back in Boston, most notably barrels of wheat flour. But they were lucky if they could use half of any given barrel of wheat that was shipped out here. Either it would be infested with weevils, or it would become wet and would be packed so hard as to be a rock. Levi Chamberlain writes in his journal about taking hammer and chisel to flour to try to get something usable out of it."

Chamberlain, who came with the second company of missionaries in 1823, was the agent in charge of doling out supplies to the mission stations on this and the other islands. He and his neighbor Sybil Bingham are two of the best sources for insights into the mission folks' daily ordeals.

When Smola leads the way to the Bing-hams' bedroom, I look at the little four-poster taking up most of the room and remember reading about a frazzled Sybil seeking refuge in it. She sniffed, "I have felt at home only by drawing my curtains around my bed. But missionary life could not be a secluded one."

Smola notes, "If you're one of the other sixteen mission stations that needed something, you had to write to Mr. Chamberlain that you needed it."

The Chamberlain files in the mission archives are full of such requests for everything from axes to tea. Smola mentions that if Chamberlain had a mission station's requested item on hand, "he'd send it on the next ship available. If not, he'd have to write back to Boston for it, which of course meant six months for his letter to get there, and six months after that for hopefully what you asked for to return here to the islands."

Dealing with the inventory (or lack thereof) and fielding the various missionaries' often cranky requests for provisions prompted Chamberlain to confide in his diary after a typical long day, "To wear out in the service of Christ is the summit of my ambition."

Chamberlain's job was so detail-oriented and so physically taxing that Hawaii gave him a newfound appreciation for Sundays, a day of rest and abstract thought. "I now perceive more than ever that the Sabbath is a blessing," he wrote. "I did not so much realize it when I was in my native country, a land of privileges; but now . . . it is a comfort to lay aside the ordinary employments and cares of the week to . . . look into eternity."

Chamberlain's descriptions of the sermons he enjoyed capture how the evangelists focused on Bible stories that spoke to their project of not only changing Hawaiians' lives but trying to keep the reformed natives from returning to their old pagan ways — drinking, gambling, dancing, fornicating, etc. He recounts one sermon on Lot's wife delivered by William Ellis, a visiting English missionary. "To explain his text," Chamberlain wrote, Ellis "alluded to the account in Genesis of the overthrow of Sodom and Gomorrah." The refugees "are to forsake their old ways . . . [and] not desire to return to their former customs and habits."

Especially disappointing to the missionaries were the relapses of two of the Hawaiian alumni of the Cornwall school. The son of the high chief of Kauai was so successful in inspiring his father, Kaumualii, to take in the missionaries and heed the call to Christ that within four months of the arrival of the *Thaddeus*, Kaumualii was writing the ABCFM a thank-you note, proclaiming, "I worship your god." But that did not stop his son from feeling, as Bingham put it, "the strong downward tendencies of a heathen community." At Kailua, William Kanui "violated his vows by excess in drinking." After Asa Thurston had him "excluded from Christian fellowship," Kanui "became a wanderer for many years."

Outside on the Mission Houses Museum grounds, Mike Smola lingers over a slab of the coral rock that was used to construct two of the mission's buildings and the gothic-style Kawaiaha'o Church across the street. "Rocks like these were quarried by hand out of the living reef out in the harbor. They were cut by hand by divers with stone and iron tools. Then the blocks were canoed to shore and used as building materials."

"Now, why coral?" Smola asks. Good question. Ever since I saw an IMAX documentary narrated by Liam Neeson at the Polynesian Cultural Center about endangered coral habitats, I can't look at the stately gray edifice of the church without hearing Neeson's Irish accent delivering apocalyptic warnings about the fate of the sea.

Smola contends, "The first reason is that the termites here are voracious, so if you want a very permanent structure, you have to find something that the termites won't eat. The other reason is that, cut into about two-foot-wide slabs like this, they made for very good insulation, keeping things cool in summer and warm in winter. By the way, some of the blocks used to build the church weigh over a thousand pounds, and it took over fourteen thousand blocks."

I have a Frommer's guidebook to Honolulu whose point-blank entry on the church claims the divers who harvested the coral "raped the reefs." By today's ecological standards, the Kawaiaha'o Church is a veritable Nanking of marine biology. Still, even if Bingham, its architect, clued in to the fact that coral reefs are colonies of living creatures sustaining underwater ecosystems, the Book of Genesis had rubber-stamped his dominion over the fish of the sea. (The church happened to be dedicated in 1842, a couple of months after Charles Darwin published *Structure and Distribution of Coral Reefs,* his first volume of findings from the voyage of the *Beagle.*)

Smola points at the Chamberlain house, mentioning it was "built in 1831 completely out of coral rock, just like the church. Now this," he says of the building's white surface, "is actually a fake brick façade here. What they did is, they made a form of lime plaster by burning coral, turning it into a paste, stuccoing over the coral, and then basically stamping the brick pattern into it."

Even if the idea of coral brick is now distasteful, it's nevertheless an aesthetically pleasing material with a bumpy, biological texture. Kawaiahaʻo is actually one of the prettiest buildings in Honolulu. That the missionaries spackled over and painted the rough surface of the coral rock on the Chamberlain house and then incised perpendicular lines in the plaster to ape the look of a New England house is somehow baffling and understandable at the same time. Plastering over the natural rock is the perfect symbol of what they hoped to do to the Hawaiians' earthy way of life.

Smola points out, "The major reason for this was that in accordance with their own beliefs they're not just mikanele for God, but also mikanele for Western ways of living. Which of course in New England means brick homes. This is a way for them to model that without actually having to make brick, which would have been fairly difficult here in the islands."

"The missionaries set up schools at every single mission station," Smola says of the cellar room where Sybil Bingham conducted hers. He continues, "Many times they had satellite schools taught by older students."

That was one of the ABCFM's shrewd moves worldwide, to increase literacy exponentially by dispatching ace pupils to a country's more remote regions.

The missionaries, Smola remarks, "focused on literacy very hard in their schools. This is mostly religiously motivated. Being good Protestants, they believed you had to be able to read the Bible for yourself in order to convert and to believe." He is referring to the Protestant Reformation's gift to the world — denying the power of priests to stand between believers and God. The Protestant mandate that each Christian, no matter how lowly, must read the Bible for him- or herself, was both a religious revolution and, more important, an educational one.

"Now, it is worth noting," Smola says, "that the mikanele did teach their schools in Hawaiian. They preached in their churches in Hawaiian, and even wrote hymns in Hawaiian, in addition to doing translation work." In fact, since Asa Thurston preached his sermons in Hawaiian, after their children were born, Lucy lobbied to keep the youngsters home on Sundays so she could offer them Sabbath teachings in English, one of her many unpaid chores.

Bingham writes in his memoir about how,

in the pulpit and in the schools, the missionaries drew on the ABCFM's earlier stateside success stories as teaching tools, particularly the biographies of Henry Obookiah and a Cherokee girl named Catherine Brown. Brown converted to Christianity when she studied at the ABCFM's first mission school in the Cherokee Nation. Following the ABCFM pattern of sending its best students farther into the hinterland to teach their countrymen, Brown signed up to teach at another Cherokee school the board established in Alabama. When Brown died of tuberculosis at the age of twenty-three, the ABCFM capitalized on her passing the same way they did Obookiah's, publishing a memoir of her conversion and subsequent piety in which she is quoted as saying, "My heart bleeds for my people" and "I cannot . . . express how much I love the missionaries with whom I live."

Bingham writes that the Hawaiian pupils found Brown's life story "encouraging . . . partly because she had been in circumstances similar to their own."

Obookiah's biography, of course, was the perfect parable. "One of the exercises from Sabbath to Sabbath," Bingham writes of the mission's early years, "was the reading and interpreting of successive portions of the memoir of Henry Opukahaia. . . . Our pupils, who had listened to the narrative with increasing interest, many of them tenderly wept."

In April of 1821, a year after the Binghams' arrival, Liholiho and Kaahumanu moved their court to Honolulu. That fall, the royal retinue voyaged to Kauai, and when they returned to Oahu, Kaahumanu brought back two new husbands — Kaumualii, the high chief of Kauai, and one of his sons (though not George from the Cornwall school). This was sort of a bad news/good news development for the missionaries, who frowned upon the father-son husband situation. Kaumualii was nevertheless one of their most promising pupils of Christianity and so they welcomed his influence on his daunting new wife, whom Bingham had described as "either heedless in regard to Christianity, or scornfully averse to our instructions." Kaumualii assured Bingham, "I have told her some things about God."

In December, Kaahumanu took so ill she was, according to Bingham, at "the borders of the grave." Sybil describes in her journal paying a visit with her husband to Kaahumanu's "sick couch." Each Bingham held a hand of the queen's and "she seemed not only willing, but desirous to hear something from the servants of the living God." Hiram was all too happy to comply, assuring the queen, "that the blessed Savior who died for sinners could preserve her body and her soul; that he could restore her to health."

The Binghams returned the next day and Sybil took to "rubbing her with spirits of camphor." When the queen asked Hiram to pray, Sybil writes, "I need not say this was a pleasant sound in our ears."

Describing his wife's soothing bedside manner, Hiram is so admiring I almost like him a little. "With unfeigned sympathy," he wrote, Sybil "bound a silken cord around [Kaahumanu's] heart, from which I think she never broke loose while she lived."

Kaahumanu's sister queen, Keopuolani, suffered a similar sickbed change of heart in 1822 and invited missionaries to preach to her in her home in Waikiki. She was a quick study, applying herself to reading and writing lessons, dismissing her second husband so that she could practice proper Christian monogamy, and turning down an old drinking buddy's offering of rum, explaining, "I am afraid of the everlasting fire."

Keopuolani's health improved by the time the second company of missionaries arrived in 1823, and she purloined a few to take

144

with her to Lahaina, a port town on Maui, the island where she was born. She built them a church and a school there. She was dead within the year, but not before issuing firm instructions to her family and the other high chiefs. She requested a proper Christian burial (instead of burning the flesh off her bones per ancient Hawaiian ritual). According to missionary William Richards, she asked, "Let my body be put in a coffin." She urged her husband to see that her son Kauikeaouli (with whom she broke the eating kapu four years earlier) and her daughter Nahi'ena'ena "should be instructed in Christianity." Her daughter, especially, the queen hoped, "may learn to love God and Jesus Christ." Richards reported that she advised her son King Liholiho, "Protect the missionaries."

Protection they would need, but Liholiho wasn't around to follow through. After his mother died, he and his favorite queen, Kamamalu, sailed to Great Britain, intent on meeting the English king. This summit never took place. Liholiho and his wife both died of measles in London.

His eleven-year-old brother, Kauikeaouli, took the name Kamehameha III. His stepmother, Queen Kaahumanu, ruled as his regent until her death in 1832.

After the Binghams personally taught
Kaahumanu to read — seated on the floor
of her thatched house, according to Hiram
— she became an official member of the
church in 1825. "Of what amazing consequence was it that Kaahumanu should be a
believer and advocate of Christianity!"
Hiram exclaimed.

Bingham noted that her approval of the
missionary endeavor sparked "the need of a
great increase of native teachers" as well as
printed matter. "Many are the people,"
Kaahumanu said. "Few are the books."
Though not for long, as the missionaries'
printing presses started cranking out Bibles,
spelling books, and the first newspaper
printed west of the Rockies.

One of the rooms in the wood home at
the Mission Houses Museum was Kaahumanu's guest room. She became, Mike
Smola says, "a very frequent visitor to the
mission station here, so much that she
referred to this room as her apartment."
One of the queen's high-necked cotton
dresses is laid out on the little rope bed,
ready to welcome her. It's the same sort of
outfit worn by the present-day Kaahumanu
Society, an organization of ladies who are
easy to pick out of a crowd at celebrations
and parades because they wear identical

black frocks in the style of the one displayed in the mission museum.

In the chronology of Hawaii's Americanization, that stuffy little room with Kaahumanu's frumpy dress is one of the landmarks, emblematic of the replacement of airy grass dwellings and airier flimsy skirts with wooden houses and long-sleeved outfits.

Five or ten years before Captain Cook arrived in Hawaii, Kaahumanu was born in a cave. The contrast between her mission house "apartment" and her rocky birthplace above Maui's Hana Bay provides a perfect education in the changes visited upon her country. Within a ten-minute walk from the mission house in Honolulu, a visitor can see the Victorian-style palace erected by later monarchs, skyscrapers of the business district, and the concrete, Nixon-era state capitol. Getting to her birthplace involves a dodgy hike up what my guidebook optimistically called a "trail." On the climb, my family and I had to cling to the branches of ironwood trees to avoid falling into the churning water below. Her birth cave, a womblike divot in the rock face, reeked of some decomposing animal. ("Don't go in there," Owen advised. "It smells like roadkill.") The bay was visible through the trees and Hawaiian men were rowing out to sea in an outrigger canoe just as they've been doing since long before baby Kaahumanu was born.

In his tour of the mission house Mike Smola says, "Now, of course the mikanele were here to spread their message of Christianity. In order to do that, you need Bibles. They very quickly determined they would like a Hawaiian-language Bible. There was an issue with this in 1820. There was no such thing as a form of written Hawaiian here in the islands. And I do emphasize *here in the islands*." He notes that back in Connecticut, Obookiah had invented an eccentric "grammar structure that used numbers to represent certain sounds."

Smola emphasizes, "The Hawaiians who lived here had a very deep, rich, and long oral tradition. Everything from memory: songs, chants, and stories detailing their history, their genealogy, their cultural stories, their religion. They also had the hula, which tells stories through dance movements, and petroglyphs, or rock carvings, rock pictures. But they didn't have an alphabet as such."

The missionaries, Smola points out, employed "the Roman alphabet we use in English. Now, the initial form of written

Hawaiian in 1822 consisted of seventeen of twenty-six English characters. Five vowels, twelve consonants. By 1826 there was an effort to standardize the written form of the language. They thought they were better served by a smaller alphabet. What they found was that several letters served the same purpose. For example B and D functioned the same as P; K the same as T; L the same as R; and B the same as W. If you look up an 1825 map of Oahu, you'll see a little tiny town on the south shore marked 'Honoruru,' as opposed to Honolulu. You also see references to 'Tamehameha,' as opposed to Kamehameha. So basically what happened was by 1826 a committee of mikanele and native Hawaiians got together and voted B, D, R, T, and V out of the alphabet, leaving us a modern Hawaiian alphabet of twelve letters. A, E, I, O, U, H, P, L, K, M, N, W.

"It took the missionaries seventeen years to translate the Bible into Hawaiian," Smola says. Partly, this is because they had so many other things to do. In Levi Chamberlain's diary, he composes entries about meetings to discuss how to go about inventing a Hawaiian grammar that are followed by entries about wrestling a 120-gallon barrel of oil into the basement. Another reason it took so long is that they were persnickety well-educated New Englanders who wanted to get it right. As Smola points out, "They did not translate it from English. They went back to the original Hebrew of the Old Testament and the Greek of the New Testament and translated that directly into Hawaiian, giving us this book, *Ke Kauoha Hou,* the Holy Scriptures. A book of 2,331 pages, it is, by the way, about twice as long as *Harry Potter and the Deathly Hallows.* And, even more amazingly, they went on to print about ten thousand copies of it."

Translating directly from Hebrew and Greek to Hawaiian speaks to the influence of the original New England clerics. The desire to train ministers capable of studying the Bible in Hebrew and Greek is the foundation of higher education in New England, and thus the United States. The Massachusetts Bay colonists, whose early ministers were mostly Cambridge-trained theologians from the old country, clamored to build a college on the outskirts of Boston to train a new generation of clergymen in those ancient tongues. And so, only six years after their arrival in the New World, they founded Harvard College in 1636. Harvard did not drop compulsory Hebrew for all students until 1755, the year John Adams graduated. Those finicky standards speak to the reason Hiram Bingham and Asa Thurston were the only members of the first company of missionaries to be called missionaries. The other men on the *Thaddeus* were deemed "assistants." Bingham and Thurston were properly ordained graduates of the new seminary at Andover. Thurston had attended Timothy Dwight's Yale before that. This preoccupation, more than racism, explains why later on the New Englanders will deny the indispensible Thomas Hopu's request to become a full-fledged minister instead of merely the missionaries' helper — not so much because he was Hawaiian but because he wasn't a seminarian.

Smola shows off the museum's replica of the Ramage printing press the missionaries brought with them on the *Thaddeus.* Besides the Bible, he says, "They also printed newspapers, hymnals, schoolbooks, government laws and proclamations, broadsides, and flyers. It's estimated that in twenty years, between 1822 and 1842, the mission presses put out over 113 million sheets of printed paper, virtually all of it in Hawaiian."

Smola says that from the first page printed in the Hawaiian islands in 1822 to the end of missionary operations in 1863, "The Hawaiian people accomplished an absolutely incredible educational feat. They went from having no written language here on the islands to seventy-five percent of all Hawaiians learning to read and write in their native language. By the way, if you factor in the slave population in the South of the United States in 1863, the literacy rate was roughly forty percent. Western Europe had a literacy rate of about sixty-five percent, which means in about forty-one years Hawaii became one of the most literate nations on the planet as a percentage of its total population. And that is perhaps the greatest accomplishment of these mikanele."

After the arrival of the second company of ABCFM missionaries, in 1823, the king and the chiefs lifted the ban on teaching commoners to read. Charles Stewart, one of the new arrivals, wrote in his journal in 1824 that the chiefs "expressly declared their intentions to have all their subjects enlightened by the *palapala* [the Hawaiian word for books and learning] and have accordingly made applications for books to distribute among them."

The printer Elisha Loomis wrote to the secretary of the ABCFM in 1825, "The demand for books has been so great. . . . A vast number of people have become able to read, and a vast number of others will be able to read by the time one of the gospels can be put into their hands."

In 1825, Kaahumanu and the high chiefs gathered in Honolulu and, according to Levi Chamberlain's journal, they "agreed to patronize instruction, and engaged to use their influence in extending it throughout the islands." They also agreed to "suppress vice, such as drunkenness, debauchery, theft and the violation of the Sabbath."

Thus within five years of their arrival the New Englanders had won over key players in the ruling class. The same cannot be said about the missionaries' peskiest opponents — their fellow Americans, the sailors.

I'm hard-pressed to find a more momentous season in the history of Hawaii than the autumn of 1819. Kealakekua Bay — the already significant Big Island cove where Captain Cook died and Henry Obookiah lit out for America — welcomed the first two New England whaling ships on September 29. Three weeks later, the first missionaries departed Boston on the *Thaddeus.* Two weeks after that the eating kapus came to an abrupt end.

Thus within five weeks during the presidency of James Monroe, Hawaii's stormy course toward becoming the fiftieth state was charted. The Hawaiian people, with their ancient balance between spiritual beliefs and earthly pleasure, were suddenly freed of or in need of an official religion, depending on one's point of view, and about to entertain swarms of haole gate-crashers representing opposing sides of America's schizophrenic divide — Bible-thumping prudes and sailors on leave. Imagine if the Hawaii Convention Center in Waikiki hosted the Values Voter Summit and the Adult Entertainment Expo simultaneously — for forty years. As Hiram Bingham put it dryly, "It has been said that the interests of the mission, and the interests of commerce, were so diverse, or opposite, that they could not flourish together."

Bingham does speak lovingly of certain American and English ships' captains, calling them "neighbors" from whom the missionaries "received repeated tokens of kindness, which alleviated the trials of our early exile." And the missionaries' diaries do record the visits of the occasional whaleman dropping by one of the mission houses in search of a Bible. Yet Bingham's fond feelings for some of the more upright sailors did not extend to their livelier shipmates, whose behavior was not necessarily "favorable to the peace, reputation or success of the missionaries, or their native helpers."

Bingham complains that the missionaries' early English lessons involved un-teaching the natives the "language of Pandemonium" they had picked up from "the frequent intercourse with an ungodly class of profane abusers of our noble English," i.e., sailors.

Remember that breakthrough night when the Binghams attended Kaahumanu's sickbed and Sybil Bingham described the "pleasant sound" of the queen asking Hiram to pray? In the same journal entry Sybil mentions that later that evening they returned home to a horrid racket, "the shameless conduct of intoxicated white men." Honolulu, she said, reminded her of "the guilty streets of Sodom."

Once the Cook expedition returned home to England in 1780, news of Hawaii spread fast, attracting steady ship traffic, mostly commercial vessels in the China trade like the one that scooped up Henry Obookiah.

Then Nantucket whale hunters discovered plentiful sperm whale fisheries off the coasts of Peru in 1818 and Japan in 1820. Located smack dab between two of the most lucrative fishing holes ever found, Hawaii in general, and Honolulu and Lahaina in particular, became the whalers' favorite stopping place, especially since Japan was closed to foreigners until 1853. The whalers visited Hawaii to refuel, pick up fresh food, water, and other supplies, air out ornery crews, and hire on new sailors, many of them native Hawaiians, to replace deserters.

In response to this influx, Hawaiian farmers started to grow more of the crops favored by sailors, such as potatoes, as well as raise more cattle, originally introduced on the islands as a gift from George Vancouver to Kamehameha I. Businesses such as stores, hotels, bars, bowling alleys, and shipping suppliers sprang up along the waterfronts. The previous barter economy, in which Hawaiians traded foodstuffs and sandalwood to sailors for Western and Asian goods, turned increasingly to cash — mostly, but not exclusively, American. "Money is beginning to be an important article," Levi Chamberlain wrote the secretary of the ABCFM in 1825. When a Nantucket whaler stopped at Lahaina in 1852, the captain's wife, Eliza Brock, wrote in her journal about shopping at a store selling "every thing beautiful of China goods, but everything is very dear here, too dear to buy much."

In 1848, the first American ship to hunt polar whales in the Arctic pulled into Honolulu Harbor. I doubt the coral-block church Hiram Bingham designed was the first place those whalemen went to brag about their feat. The subsequent fashionable if miserable business of arctic whaling soon made Hawaii's subtropical ports all the more alluring to the frostbitten crews.

Until the first petroleum well was drilled in Pennsylvania in 1859, whale oil *was* oil. In *Leviathan,* a fine history of whaling, Eric Jay Dolin enumerates whale oil's manifold applications: "It was used in the production of soap, textiles, leather, paints, and varnishes, and it lubricated the tools and machines that drove the Industrial Revolution." In fact, its use as a lubricant impervious to extremes in temperature persisted well into the space age — NASA lubed its moon landers and other remotely operated vehicles with sperm whale oil until the International Whaling Commission banned commercial whaling in 1986.

"To the whalemen," Dolin asserts, "whales were swimming profit centers to be taken advantage of, not preserved." He talks up ambergris, "a byproduct of irritation in a sperm whale's bowel" as the ingredient that "gave perfumes great staying power and was worth its weight in gold." A lady who dabbed floral-scented whale bowel irritant behind her ears also cinched whalebone around her waist. "The baleen cut from the mouths of whales," Dolin points out, "shaped the course of feminine fashion by putting the hoop in hooped skirts and giving form to stomach-tightening and chest-crushing corsets." Baleen was also used in umbrellas. A text panel at the Whalers Village Museum in Lahaina calls it "the true forerunner to plastic."

In the nineteenth century, Dolin boasts, "American whale oil lit the world." He notes, "Spermaceti, the waxy substance from the heads of sperm whales, produced the brightest- and cleanest-burning candles the world has ever known."

Imagine a Bostonian in 1851 sitting by the fire in his Beacon Hill parlor, trying to make sense of a strange new novel called *Moby-Dick.* He comes to the passage in which the sailor narrating the book brags about "us whale hunters" how "almost all tapers, lamps, and candles that burn round the globe, burn, as before so many shrines, to our glory!" This reader must have glanced sideways at the table next to his chair and stared at the whale-oil lamp or the whale-oil candle illuminating the page he was on. How many times must he have looked upon his reading light in wonder, or horror, as he progressed through Melville's weird yarns of whale butchery? Especially after perusing the homoerotic paragraph in chapter 94 when Ishmael, along with his swarthy ship-mates, was elbow deep in a vat of sper-maceti trying to squeeze the hardened sludge back into liquid form (because it cools and hardens postmortem). Ishmael swoons over this orgy of greasy squeezing, sometimes clasping and stroking his cowork-ers' hands beneath the slime: "Let us all squeeze ourselves into each other; let us squeeze ourselves universally into the very milk and sperm of kindness." Could a genteel reader ever light his spermaceti candles again without blushing?

Melville, himself a former hand on the whale ship *Acushnet,* captured whaling's glories and horrors — the tyranny of its captains, the racial variety and bravery of its crews, the excitement of harpooning and the hellish fires heating the try-pots, those colossal iron cauldrons of boiling oil, their noxious fires fueled by hacked-up whale bits used as kindling. As a display at the Whal-ers Village Museum puts it, "The whale was literally cooking itself on the flames of its own blubber."

Considering that it is located within a La-haina mall with a store called Island Cutie, a shopper who wanders into the Whalers

Village Museum can learn a thing or two: processing a whale takes a couple of days and "could yield up to 2,000 gallons of oil"; the ship *Sarah* sailed home to Nantucket with "almost 3,500 barrels of sperm oil on one voyage worth $89,000"; "a single try-pot could render two hundred gallons of oil per hour." Also, "injured sailors faced the horror of surgery performed by ship masters using carpentry and sail making tools."

The museum displays a replica of a fore-castle, the dark, dirty sleeping quarters below deck. There men were shoehorned into grim little bunk beds infested with fleas and lice. As a sufferer of claustrophobia and seasickness, I can barely look at the creepy forecastle exhibit without dry-heaving.

Most whaling ships were based out of New England, and most of those from New Bedford, Massachusetts, where, Ralph Waldo Emerson wrote, "they hug an oil-cask like a brother."

I stopped by New Bedford on one of those perfect New England October days, when the sky is blue and the leaves are gilded and the air has that bracing autumnal bite so that all you want to do is bob for apples or hang a witch or something.

I came to visit the New Bedford Whaling Museum, but really the whole town is a whaling museum. At the National Park Service's visitor center I chatted with the volunteer manning the information booth. I asked her if she had ever attended the town's annual *Moby-Dick* marathon, in which the novel is read aloud straight through, all night long. Kind of a dream of mine to witness that. She winced, blurting, "No! I've never read *Moby-Dick* all the way through. I don't care for it. It's not my taste." I found this hilarious and egged her on, said I guess we wouldn't be discussing our favorite chapters, mine being the one about the sermon delivered in the chapel a couple of blocks away. She pointed out the window at passersby and griped, "People around here rhapsodize about it day after day!" Then she asked me if I needed any help and I told her I came in to get a map I had heard about and she asked me which one and I said, "Herman Melville's New Bedford." She handed it to me, shaking her head.

I popped in the Seaman's Bethel, the aforementioned chapel where Melville had an old sea captain turned minister give his whopper of a sermon to whalemen about to ship out. I sat in the pew where the young Melville once sat. It's a nice little church, its walls lined with tributes to men lost at sea. But the place is marred by the phony, cartoonish ship-shaped pulpit the town put there after the John Huston movie of *Moby-Dick* came out in 1956 and tourists showed up expecting to see the stupid movie prop Orson Welles stood behind to deliver the sermon. I know sixteen-year-olds who have never heard of Bill Murray, much less John Huston; I think it's safe to say visitors' Huston-movie expectations have dwindled to the point where the real pulpit can be once again restored. Then maybe they could haul the boaty lectern to the visitor center. The only thing funnier than a New Bedford tourism ambassador who hates *Moby-Dick* would be a New Bedford tourism ambassador denouncing *Moby-Dick* from the pulpit of *Moby-Dick* the movie.

Moving along, past the house where Frederick Douglass lived for a spell after his escape from slavery, I ambled up to the Greek Revival mansion the whaling merchant William Rotch, Jr., built in 1834. Admiring its shuttered windows, columned porch, polished antiques, and sumptuous carpets, I thought of the grimy sailors whose sweat paid for such finery and how they drank and whored through Lahaina, or tried to. Of the splendid homes like Rotch's, Melville noted that "all these brave houses and flowery gardens came from the Atlantic, Pacific, and Indian oceans. One and all, they were harpooned and dragged up hither from the bottom of the sea."

The captains in the employ of Rotch and his fellow merchants passed through the Doric columns of the Customs House on their way in and out of town. Built in 1836, and designed by the architect of the Washington Monument, it's still the oldest operating customs house in the country. A plaque points out, "Here ship captains walked up the granite steps to register their crews and declare their cargoes before they were granted clearance to leave or enter the port." Because it is still a federal building, a portrait of the president of the United States hangs in the hallway inside. I can't help but wonder what those old captains would think if they saw the picture and learned that the president was born in Honolulu, now a state capital.

When those captains walked out of the Customs House toward the waterfront, they did so with the knowledge that they wouldn't be declaring any cargo for three or four years, the average length of a whaling voyage.

By the time the captains and their crews were given their first leave in Polynesia they

163

had usually been at sea for a year or more. The sailors came ashore malnourished, flea-bitten, and flogged, ships' captains maintaining discipline with the crack of the whip. For some of them, jumping ship in subtropical islands proved too tantalizing to resist. This included Herman Melville, who, despite his epic mash notes to the whaleman's life, ditched his ship, *Acushnet,* in the Marquesas Islands, hiding in the hinterlands until the ship finally left without him. He made his way to Honolulu, where he worked in one of the bowling alleys where his fellow miscreant sailors amused themselves. Then he went home and wrote, among other books, *Moby-Dick.* It flopped and he worked as a customs inspector in New York until he died.

Because of this persistent parade of deadbeats washing ashore, going AWOL in Hawaii was illegal. Not that that stopped sailors from sticking around. I've been to the old prison in Lahaina. It has a sunny courtyard shaded by palms. Even lockup in Hawaii was preferable to the floating jails the men had forsaken.

After months if not years of monotony on board a whale ship, long stretches of boredom in between the occasional panicky whale hunt followed by the stench of burning blubber — after being cooped up with filthy, farting, masturbating shipmates, enduring the captain's beatings, the sickening food, the rancid water — it goes without saying that a whaleman pulling into Lahaina or Honolulu was going to want to blow off some steam. Perhaps grab a drink with one hand and a girl with the other.

The last thing a sailor wanted to see on shore was "a tall, dark-looking man, with a commanding eye, thin lips and a clean shaven face," as William Thomes described the missionary who came to rescue him from fun. Thomes, a deserter, had been hiding out in a happy little native enclave on Oahu. He had settled into the contented village rhythms of fishing and eating fruit. The missionary, informing Thomes he was breaking the law by abandoning his ship without government consent, nagged, "You are living here in idleness and sin, I suppose."

In the four decades the Sandwich Islands Mission lasted, which happened to coincide with whaling's golden age, the ABCFM dispatched twelve boatloads of ministers from New England harbors. Hawaiian ports hosted six hundred whaleships in 1846 alone.

This influx was especially apparent in Lahaina, a small, charming city a few streets deep nestled between an excellent harbor and the West Maui Mountains. Nowadays, cruise ships pull in there instead of whalers but the effect is similar in terms of head count, if not physical appearance. I happened to be downtown one day when a *Princess* cruise ship let loose scores of elderly looky-loos. These retirees were certainly cleaner than the whalemen of yore, and most of them were excited about historic walking tours instead of booze or trysts, but it was still a flash flood of haoles pouring down the narrow streets.

Wildly outnumbered by seamen, the missionaries nevertheless had the ear of the government, whom they persuaded to limit liquor sales and outlaw not just prostitution but fornication in general.

One of the earliest publications of the printing press at the Honolulu mission house was a handbill decreed by the king (under missionary advice) on March 8, 1822. To wit:

Whereas disturbances have arisen of late on shore, the peace broken and the inhabitants annoyed, by the crews of different vessels having liberty granted them on shore, it is hereby ordered by

His Majesty the King, that in future, should any seamen of whatever vessel, be found riotous or disturbing the peace in any manner, he or they shall be immediately secured in the Fort, where he or they shall be detained until thirty dollars is paid for the release of each offender.

As the missionaries gained more and more influence over Queen Kaahumanu, the other high chiefs, and, eventually, the king, the prohibitions against sailors' bad behavior multiplied and got more amusingly specific. Arrest statistics posted at the old prison in Lahaina for convictions on Maui, Molokai, and Lanai in 1855 include 335 cases of drunkenness, 111 counts of adultery and fornication, 49 for breaking the Sabbath, 21 for profanity, 14 for "disturbing the quiet of the night," and, my personal favorite, 89 cases of "furious riding," which is to say, speeding on horseback.

At the New Bedford Whaling Museum, I watched a film whose narrator noted that the whalers "find themselves taking America to where it had never been before." That statement is even truer in Hawaii, where the sailors as well as the missionaries, most of them born within 150 miles of Boston

Harbor, established a new front of America's time-honored culture war halfway around the world. "Evidently the Pacific was a Boston suburb," Earl Derr Biggers wrote in 1925.

The conflict between Saturday night and Sunday morning is older than New England. English immigrants to that region during the Great Migration from 1620 to 1640 were divided into "saints and strangers," the Pilgrims and Puritans who exiled themselves to farm and worship God versus their secular fellow travelers, many of them fishermen, whose taverns soon outnumbered the churches. One of the godly condemned his saltier fisherfolk neighbors as "beastly, barbarous, belching drunkards."

To pious New Englanders agriculture was culture. The word the English used to describe their colonies was "plantation." When Samuel J. Mills, Jr., brought Henry Obookiah home to his minister father's Connecticut farm, Mills Sr. swooned over how handy Obookiah was with a sickle, speedy reaping apparently indicating good moral character. One reason the ABCFM approved the layman Daniel Chamberlain's appointment in the pioneer missionary company was his background as a farmer. The board believed he would lead the charge in achieving the mission's goal of "covering those islands with fruitful fields." Of course, the islands were already covered in fruitful fields of actual fruit, as well as taro and sweet potatoes, the Hawaiians being expert horticulturists already. The natives had even mastered growing taro, a wetland crop, in the islands' dry plains.

Chamberlain, his skills superfluous, took ill, along with his wife. When they decided to move with their five children back to the United States in 1823, their voyage home ended with a lawsuit, *Chamberlain v. Chandler.* But it might as well have been called *Saint v. Stranger,* considering how perfectly it symbolized the cultural divide between New England's fishers and fishers of men.

According to an account in the periodical *The Missionary Herald,* the Chamberlains' skipper, one Captain Chandler, "cherished a most malignant hatred of missionaries. . . . During nearly the whole voyage, he was guilty of gross abuse towards Mr. Chamberlain, his wife and children. This abuse was principally confined to language." In short, the Chamberlains spent the entire trip being cussed at. They sued, winning $400 in damages for mental suffering.

The years 1826 and '27 marked the nadir

of missionary-seaman relations. The Sandwich Islands section of the ABCFM's annual report in 1827 tiptoes up to its chronicle of disturbing anecdotes. The mortified report states that in Hawaii, "a series of events took place, which, for the honor of our country and of Christendom, the Committee would gladly pass over in silence."

In January of 1826 the demure chronicle contends that the *Dolphin,* a United States military ship, arrived in Honolulu. "Her commander expressed his regret at the existence of a law, prohibiting females from visiting ships on an infamous errand." Learning of Hiram Bingham's influence, and determined to procure female companionship for himself and his shipmates, the captain informed the high chiefs "that unless the law against prostitution were repealed, he would come and tear down the houses of the missionaries."

Six or seven members of the *Dolphin*'s crew burst into a religious service Bingham was conducting at a chief's house and threatened him with clubs. Then they went off and broke some windows at the mission house. When the captain arrived on the scene, rather than apologize for his men's threats and vandalism he purported that "he had rather have his hands tied behind him, or even cut off, and go home to the United States mutilated, than to have it said, that the privilege of having prostitutes on board his vessel was denied him."

Some of the chiefs, scared or fed up with the conflict, secretly spirited a few willing ladies on board the ship anyway. At which point, the report concedes, "in the dusk of the evening, a shout ran from one deck to another as if a glorious victory had been achieved." That night, the report admits, "Hell rejoiced, and angels covered their faces in grief."

The same report notes that Honolulu Harbor received more than a hundred ships that year. The presence of a couple of thousand sailors loitering on shore resulted in horse races, card playing, and a return "to the songs and dances of former times." Nevertheless, the account goes on to boast, the Sandwich Islands Mission printed ten thousand copies of a book of hymns that year. So take that, songs of former times.

A year later, in Lahaina, the governor of Maui — Hoapili, the late Queen Keopuolani's final husband — held the American captain of the English whaler *John Palmer* until his crew returned native women who were on board breaking the law forbidding prostitution. The crew, writes the ABCFM's Rufus Anderson, "opened a fire upon the town, throwing five cannon-balls into it, all in the direction of the mission-house." Luckily nothing but feelings were hurt in the incident.

The whalers stopped over in Hawaii mainly in the fall and spring. This seasonal schedule tended to exaggerate the moral backsliding the missionaries constantly complained about, especially in Lahaina. The Maui Mission Station reports in the 1830s are rife with church members being suspended for adultery and drunkenness. One man exhibited "general unchristian deportment and contempt of those who went to converse with him." One report notes that because of the ship traffic, "The children of Lahaina, while they have enjoyed superior advantages, have also superior temptations to encounter."

The Nantucket whaling captain's wife, Eliza Brock, captured Lahaina's contradictions in her journal. The streets, she noticed on a stopover in 1854, were "thronged all day long with . . . sailors on shore on liberty." Nevertheless, she attended a church service led by the ABCFM's missionary Dwight Baldwin and was "quite delighted their worship is very solemn."

Mrs. Brock's journal also noted that her husband's whale hunt, like all whale hunts in the 1850s, was progressing slowly because the creatures "are not easily captured as in times gone by." Whaling's triumph was the root of its demise. The New Englanders had slaughtered so many whales that quarry was becoming ever more scarce.

In 1850, a Honolulu newspaper for sailors, *The Friend,* published an odd letter supposedly written by a polar whale. Pondering his kind's impending annihilation at the hands of "whale killing monsters" from New Bedford, Sag Harbor, and New London, the whale pleads, "I write on behalf of my butchered and dying species. . . . Must we all be murdered in cold blood? Must our race become extinct?"

When I took my nephew Owen to the Whalers Village Museum in Lahaina, he kept coming up to me to issue irate outbursts. "They shouldn't kill whales!" and "I can't believe they killed so many whales!" He looked at the harpoons hanging on the wall and shook his head. I told him to cheer up, that soon enough the whales would be in luck because the whole world was about to go ape for fossil fuels. "Good!" he said.

The Pennsylvania petroleum boom of the 1860s slowed down sperm whales' extinction. A political cartoon in an 1861 issue of *Vanity Fair* shows whales dressed up in tuxedos and ball gowns, sipping champagne under banners proclaiming "Oils well that ends well" and "We wail no more for our blubber." The caption reads: "Grand ball given by the whales in honor of the discovery of the oil wells in Pennsylvania."

Hawaii's commercial fortunes would have suffered along with whaling's decline if not for the triumphant rise of sugar agriculture spurred on by the American Civil War. It's poetic that some of the early Hawaiian sugar entrepreneurs boiled their cane in iron try-pots the whalers left behind. I once spotted some try-pots repurposed yet again on the grounds of a plush resort on Maui — as planters full of exotic foliage. Nearly two centuries of Hawaiian economics bloomed from that kettle, from whaling, to sugar, to tourism.

When Kamehameha's heir, Liholiho, decided to make his ill-fated state visit to Great Britain in 1823, he sailed on an English whaleship captained by Valentine Starbuck, a member of a venerable Nantucket whaling family (whose name Melville would appropriate for the *Pequod*'s first mate in *Moby-Dick*). In 1825, Liholiho and his wife, struck dead by measles, returned home to Hawaii in ornate coffins on HMS *Blonde,* a British Royal Navy frigate under the command of the seventh Lord Byron, cousin of the sixth Lord Byron, the late poet. Along with the royals' remains, the ship brought tidings from King George IV denying British control of Hawaiian internal affairs but promising the islands friendship and protection.

Robert Dampier, an artist aboard the *Blonde,* described the Honolulu funeral procession for the royal couple. The coffins were rowed ashore from the frigate in small boats. Cannons were fired and a Hawaiian honor guard bearing muskets lined the road to the mission church. "They were all clothed in English dresses of various date, size, and manufacture," wrote Dampier, "and many lacking in that essential part of a soldier's accoutrements, a pair of Trousers."

The procession "was headed by nine Sandwichers accoutered in their beautiful war cloaks" bearing standards, followed by the band from the *Blonde* playing a death march; the American missionaries; the ship's chaplain and surgeon; forty noble pallbearers lugging the coffins; the young King Kauikeaouli; his little sister, Princess

Nahiʻenaʻena (on the arm of Lord Byron); Kaahumanu (on the arm of the British first lieutenant); more chiefs; and the naval officers, "clad in their dress uniforms." Dampier opined that "As they all tramped thus solemnly along, the whole group formed a striking and interesting Spectacle." Indeed, a pageant of Polynesian royalty, a brass band, pantsless guards, and Lord Byron's cousin seems like a fanciful tableau from some arcane folk ballad Joan Baez might have recorded in 1962.

The published account, *Voyage of H.M.S. Blonde to the Sandwich Islands*, written by Lord Byron and his shipmates, remarks that "We could not help reflecting on the strange combination of circumstances here before us: every thing native-born and ancient in the Isles was passing away."

At a somber gathering at Prime Minister Kalanimoku's house, described in *Voyage of the H.M.S. Blonde*, King Kauikeaouli and Princess Nahiʻenaʻena observed the proceedings from a sofa. The boy was between ten and twelve years old and his sister a couple of years younger. They were "in European suits of mourning, and seated on a beautiful feather garment, which some of the affectionate natives had woven [for the princess]."

Hawaiian feather-work like the twenty-foot-long sarong the princess was sitting on was — and is — revered for its magnificence. The feather capes and cloaks made for the chiefs, composed of elegant geometric designs in yellow, black, and red, are masterpieces of design and handicraft.

"The feathers of birds were the most valued possessions of the ancient Hawaiians," wrote David Malo. The ruling class employed bird catchers to trap birds like the mamo and the oʻo to pluck their feathers. These feathers were tied into netting to construct the nobles' capes and feather helmets, which they wore on ceremonial occasions and in battle. The gorgeous yellow cloak woven of nearly half a million mamo feathers that belonged to Kamehameha the Great and is now in the collection of Honolulu's Bishop Museum is a Hawaiian national treasure.

As John Dominis Holt wrote in his 1964 meditation *On Being Hawaiian,* "I am filled with an aesthetic pleasure when I think of tall chiefs wearing feather covered helmets; great cloaks and capes — again, of feathers — draped across their shoulders, or covering the full length of their frames as they walked across the land."

On Being Hawaiian was one of the early

landmarks of a movement in the 1960s and seventies now called the Hawaiian Renaissance, a reawakening of appreciation for and interest in Hawaiian language and culture. In his remarkable paragraph on the featherwork, Holt manages a museumgoer's rare feat: truly seeing an artifact on display. He appreciates the sociology of the textiles — their fascinating political, cultural, and ecological context — but he does that without forgetting to look upon them as art. Art is made by individuals, not societies. Holt proclaims, "I see these objects in the Bishop Museum today, and marvel at the workmanship of Neolithic craftsmen, and the artistic insight that led to the conceptualization of the feather cloak and helmet as garments of state. The element of extreme grace is apparent in the Hawaiian featherwork objects."

According to David Malo, Kamehameha issued an order to the trappers to protect these species to ensure they would survive to adorn his children: " 'When you catch the birds do not strangle them. Take what feathers you want and let them go to grow more.' " Holt alludes to this in his essay, remarking, "All the lore of bird-catchers, which tells of their methods of taking feathers from live birds, is manifest of a sophisticated understanding of conservation, which extended throughout the whole of classic Hawaiian Society."

As the plumage on the o'o was overwhelmingly black, the catchers were able to extract a bird's small number of yellow feathers and set it free. I say "were" because the o'o and the mamo are now extinct, due to a number of factors, including hunting, changes in their Big Island habitat brought about by cattle ranching, and diseases that may have been borne by invasive species like the mosquito that arrived as stowaways on foreign ships.

In *Hawaii's Story by Hawaii's Queen,* Liliuokalani describes three pairs of o'o birds she sent to friends on Kauai, hoping to replenish the species "under whose wings may be found the choice yellow feathers used in the manufacture of cloaks or collars exclusively pertaining to the Hawaiian chiefs of high rank." Delighted to hear that one pair of the birds was "thriving," she attributed their vigor to a flowering mimosa shrub near her friends' house. "They are true Hawaiians," she wrote of the birds. "Flowers are necessary for their very life."

The queen hoped that the birds would continue to flourish. But the feather-work birds were already nearly extinct by 1898, the year her book was published to argue against American annexation. The queen's contemporary, the ornithologist Henry Wetherbee Henshaw cited 1898 as the point of no return for the o'o; it was also the year the birdwatcher spotted the last mamo he ever saw.

The Bishop Museum safeguards the o'o feather skirt of Nahi'ena'ena in a climate-controlled storage facility. It can only be seen by special appointment. When I was ushered into the cold, white room where the skirt was partially unfurled, a security guard watched over me. I had only seen examples of old feather-work on cloaks secured behind glass in the museum's Hawaiian Hall or on display in Iolani Palace. Up close, its texture is downright luscious, a field of legal-pad yellow ever so flecked with hints of black and red. One edge is decorated with black and red triangles that used to line each end. (After the princess's death, it was cut in half and sewn back together and used to drape over the caskets of kings. There are photographs of it blanketing the coffin of King Kalakaua in 1891.)

Nahi'ena'ena's skirt, the longest piece of feather-work ever made, was a symbol of her unique status, a tribute to her power. Artisans constructed her feather skirt for her to wear to meet her brother Liholiho upon his return from England. In *The Journal of the Polynesian Society,* John Charlot argues persuasively that the idea was, she would greet her brother in the fetching garment to signify their impending procreation. If the weavers' intent was to beguile the king, then I can report that it takes all my decorum, all the archival protocol drilled into me during the museum internships of my youth, to restrain myself from running my hands over the skirt's downy surface. I tell the guard that it looks so soft and inviting I want to curl up in it and take a nap. He tells me not to.

A chant about the hoped-for coupling of Nahi'ena'ena and Liholiho proposes, "Clinging chiefs, laid down in delight. / The chief clings, this earth endures." This was the weight bearing down on the little girl's narrow shoulders: she must bear her brother's children to save the Hawaiian world.

The Hawaiian population in 1778 when Captain Cook landed in Kauai has been estimated at over 300,000. The 1890 census recorded 34,436 pure Hawaiians. As with natives of the Americas after European contact, the runaway death rate can be attributed to outbreaks of smallpox, cholera, influenza, typhoid (which killed Henry

Obookiah), measles (which killed Liholiho and his wife), and venereal disease.

In 1825, the year of Liholiho's funeral, missionary wife Mercy Whitney bemoaned the situation: "The mortality of this nation is a motive which ought to excite us to steady persevering and self-denying labors for their good."

On the one hand, the missionaries' crusade to prohibit Hawaiian women from engaging in prostitution and fornication with visiting disease-ridden seamen probably saved lives. On the other hand, since their countrymen started dropping like flies after the haoles showed up, some natives suspected the missionaries' religion was to blame for the higher body count. In an essay in the Bishop Museum archives entitled "Mistaken Ideas Concerning the Missionaries," written by an unidentified Lahaina student in 1842, the essayist takes a look back at initial fears about the New Englanders. After Hiram Bingham built the first church on Oahu, the student recalls, "When it was completed some of the natives said among themselves, 'That house of worship built by the haoles is a place in which they will pray us all to death. It is meant to kill us.'"

In her book about the missionary wives,

Pilgrim Path, Mary Zwiep describes the zeitgeist of the 1820s, arguing that some Hawaiians feared that "disease or death was the price being exacted for their association with the missionaries." When William Richards wrote from Lahaina in June 1824 that ten out of thirty high chiefs had died within the past two years, he admitted: "Some say it is the *palapala.*" Palapala means papers, books, and learning in general but especially the Bible.

Richards, who accompanied Princess Nahi'ena'ena on a tour of Maui when she was thirteen, wrote down her remarks to her subjects in a remote east coast village where the inhabitants were wary of their new school. Addressing the villagers' fears of the Scriptures, she compared the more autocratic ancient high chiefs to those of her generation. "Formerly we were the terror of the country — when visiting your district we should perhaps have bidden you erect a heiau, and after being worn out with this labor, we should have sacrificed you in it. Now we bring you the *palapala* — the word of God. Why should you fear it?"

When the princess's feather skirt was unveiled in 1825, even grumpy Hiram Bingham could appreciate its beauty, if not its intent, describing it as "a splendid yellow feather *pau,* or robe, nine yards in length and one in breadth, manufactured with skill and taste, at great expense."

Calling the pa'u a "robe" as Bingham did is a mistake I made myself in a conversation with Noelle Kahanu, who works in the education department at the Bishop Museum. "It's a skirt!" she corrected me.

The skirt, as a covering for the hips and genitals, represents the princess's power to procreate, to continue the royal line.

The princess understood this, which is why at the gathering attended by sailors from the *Blonde* she was sitting on top of the feathers, wearing a stiff black dress instead. The *Blonde* arrived in 1825, two years after her mother, Queen Keopuolani, issued deathbed instructions that Nahi'ena'ena should be taught to love and obey Christ. So the princess had spent a lot of time in the company of the missionaries in Lahaina. However, most of her guardians and entourage were Hawaiian traditionalists. Much like an immigrant's daughter, she lived in two worlds and daily moved between them.

The Lahaina missionaries, especially William Richards, lectured the princess that the Bible forbids giving birth to sons and daughters who were also her nieces and nephews. Richards, a native of Plainfield, Massachusetts, graduated from Williams College (where the Haystack Meeting would spark what became the ABCFM) and Andover Seminary (where Bingham and Thurston studied and where Yale's Timothy Dwight preached the founding sermon that proclaimed, *"the islands of the sea, already wait for his law"*). Thus at the very moment the princess was heeding a voice trained in the elite epicenters of New England Protestantism, Lahaina artists were weaving a million feathers into a twenty-five-foot-long fertility symbol so she could prolong the ancient Hawaiian way of life.

Traditional Hawaiian skirts were worn topless. Nahi'ena'ena was only comfortable in haole attire, and not only for moral reasons. Western clothing had been a fad among the Hawaiians, especially the high chiefs, since the arrival of Captain Cook. Which is why the prime minister, Kalanimoku, greeted the missionaries on the *Thaddeus* in yellow silk pants he had acquired from Western sailors. According to *Voyage of H.M.S. Blonde,* Lord Byron presented Nahi'ena'ena's brother, the king, with a British military uniform and the boy "instantly put it on, and strutted about the whole morning in ecstasy."

The missionary Charles Stewart recounted that when the princess was presented with the feather skirt, she ran away from it, escaping to the mission house. He wrote, "She wept so as scarcely to be pacified by us, and returned to the chiefs only in time to take her seat, and have it thrown carelessly about her over her European dress." The *Blonde* report concurs, noting, "The little girl has been so long under the tuition of the missionaries, that she . . . absolutely refuses ever to appear in the native costume; so that the *pau* was used today merely as a covering for her seat."

European expeditions, such as those of Cook and La Pérouse, often employed artists to document the people and landscapes encountered at sea. The ship's artist of the *Blonde,* Robert Dampier, convinced some of the chiefs to sit for portraits. He had the following "difficulty to wrestle with. I wished my Friends to array themselves in their Country's Costume; this desire they treated as most unreasonable, and came decked out in their best black silk gowns." In the striking pair of paintings he made of King Kauikeaouli and Princess Nahiʻenaʻena now hanging in the Honolulu Academy of Arts, Dampier nevertheless draped the young royals in traditional red, yellow, and black feather cloaks.

Americans get blamed for the American-ization of Hawaii, and deservedly so. But the gentlemen from the *Blonde,* eyeball wit-nesses of the transition, testify to the Hawai-ian chiefs' willful collaboration in that process. Dampier, the English painter, faked his portraits of the royal siblings to make them look more Hawaiian, painting them in traditional feather cloaks even though they were wearing fashionable silk and wool. Decades before the missionaries' offspring plotted to end the Hawaiian Kingdom, the Hawaiian ruling class voluntarily dropped some of the old ways. For instance, Kaahu-manu issued an edict forbidding the hula in 1830 (though people ignored it after she died, a couple of years later).

Still, in the 1820s, even the most pro-Christian, silk-clad chiefs still clung might-ily to this tradition: the celebration of royal incest.

At the time of their brother's funeral, Kauikeaouli was around twelve years old and the princess was eight to ten. There is much gossip (but no evidence) that by this early age brother and sister were already sleeping together, per the Hawaiian custom. Previously, the mission's printer, Elisha Loomis, commented that the royal children's incestuous romance "would appear extraordinary in America, as the prince is but ten years of age and the princess less than 7 or 8. It should be remembered, however, that the persons arrive at the age of puberty here much sooner than in a colder climate." He adds, "Chastity is not a recommendation" for Hawaiian boys and girls, "the sexes associating without restraint almost from infancy."

Now that their brother the king had died, the two children were the islands' two highest-ranking of the high chiefs, the only surviving offspring of Kamehameha the Great and his sacred wife, Keopuolani, daughter of a brother-sister marriage. According to the old ways, the royal siblings' union was to be applauded. A marriage between them was hoped for, planned on. In fact, the chiefs held a meeting in Lahaina in 1824 to debate the propriety of a marriage between the siblings in light of the missionaries' pleas against it.

Elisha Loomis took part in the discussion. He reported that the generally Christian-leaning Kalanimoku

asked me if it was proper for a brother and sister to live together as man and wife. Of course I told him it was not. He

188

said it was a common practice in this country. I informed him and the others present that it was forbidden in the word of God, it was disallowed in civilised communities, and that barrenness or weak and sickly children were effects of such improper connexions, an effect which might be noticed even in the beasts of the field. They all seemed to admit of the correctness of these re-marks. . . . They feel a difficulty in regard to the case in hand. There are no two persons of suitable age of equal rank with the princess. . . . Kaikeoeua said the offspring of two such Chiefs as the prince and princess would be an "[alii] nui roa," a very great chief. We replied, "True, but if they (a brother and a sister) are united, it is highly probable they will have no children." We asked them if they had ever known an instance where chil-dren had sprung from the union of a brother and sister. They mentioned Ke-opuolani, mother of the prince and princess, she being the child of parents who were brother and sister. We told them we knew of that fact, but that Ke-opuolani was an only child and weakly. She finally died at an early age. The prince is looked upon as successor to

[Liholiho] and it is thought desirable he should have a wife of high rank, that the royal blood may not be contaminated.

Noelle Kahanu from the Bishop Museum told me, "Theirs was the last sibling marriage ever proposed in the history of our kingdom. I think it's important to not judge the decisions of our [chiefs] by today's standards — that's the easy thing. What's difficult is putting ourselves in their place — we can't even begin to imagine the difficulties, the challenges, the hardships. They did the best they could, and they made decisions and choices that they thought were best for themselves and their people."

Here is a snippet of a conversation I had with a Honolulu-born friend in which I confessed that the image of an eight-year-old Nahi'ena'ena sleeping with her brother made me want to call a social worker.

Her: We don't have to say, "That's good, that's bad," just, "That's so totally different."

Me: I think it's a little bad.

Her: Well, I do too. But they were decent people.

The foundation of royalty is the notion that one family's blood is better than any other's and therefore needs to be protected from being, as that Hawaiian chief put it, "contaminated." The way said contamination is prevented is through inbreeding, which, of course, is often the genetic cause of a royal dynasty's demise through sterility, miscarriages, stillbirths, and sickliness. That would be true of the heirs of Keopuolani just as it was true of the House of Hapsburg. Nahiʻenaʻena's brother probably fathered the one child she would bear, and that infant lived only a few hours, and she herself died a couple of months after that.

Nahiʻenaʻena embodies what Hawaii became: pulled apart. Queen Liliuokalani, born in 1838, two years after Nahiʻenaʻena's death, thus came of age in the hybrid Hawaii and would manage to balance her Christian beliefs and native pride with authority. But Nahiʻenaʻena spent her short conflicted life lurching back and forth between the old ways and those of the New Englanders, sometimes taking refuge in the Church, sometimes in her brother's arms, and, more and more as she got older, in liquor. She even had two weddings — a traditional ceremony in which she wedded her brother in the presence of the highest chiefs, and a Christian service in which she gave her hand to a man the missionaries approved of. During her pregnancy, she chose to stay with her brother, and went to Honolulu, where the old guard awaited the birth of the heir, a little boy who died the day he was born. When Nahi'ena'ena died, soon thereafter, she was only around twenty years old.

The missionaries had hovered over the princess's deathbed, hoping to coax her final repentance. In his remembrance of her, Hiram Bingham, while inferring she was under Satan's spell, could not conceal his fondness for the deceased. He wrote, "This beautiful flower, once the pride of the nation, and once the joy of the infant church of Lahaina, having been blighted, through the power of the great enemy, was now cut down, and passed away."

The chance for a royal child of sacred rank died with her. Her brother was the last surviving chief to hold that rank. Noelle Kahanu told me, "Kauikeaouli was indeed the last divine king, the last who lived like his ancestors."

At Nahi'ena'ena's Honolulu funeral, her feather skirt was displayed atop her coffin, just as it would one day swaddle the casket of Kalakaua, the last king, fifty-five years later.

I have a hula dancer friend from Maui,

John-Mario Sevilla, who told me about viewing the princess's skirt at the Bishop Museum as part of a hula conference. He said that when he and his fellow dancers saw it, "The Hawaiians in the group wept." Nahi'ena'ena's skirt was woven as a symbol of fertility and birth, but because of her sad, short life, and because the Kamehameha line would die out and the monarchy was overthrown, it is now a fluffy yellow symbol of loss.

When the Lahaina church excommunicated Nahi'ena'ena in 1835, the clergy dispatched David Malo to break the news to the princess. According to Levi Chamberlain, Malo found her on board a ship, drinking — her increasing drunkenness being one of the reasons the church was severing its ties. Given the demands upon her soul, who wouldn't choose liquor's oblivion? She would be dead within a year. Malo and the princess, both of them protégés of the missionary William Richards, personify the upheaval of their changing times. But if the princess lost herself somewhere in all the jostling, David Malo, commuting between worlds, found his voice.

Leimana Brimeyer, one of Malo's descendants, told me, "David Malo was twenty-seven at the time of the 'Western invasion' in 1820, but he already had an insatiable quest for knowledge. Meeting new people from a faraway land just added fuel to the fire. He met Reverend William Richards in 1823. He essentially took David Malo under his wing and taught him how to read and write. Although David Malo never quite mastered the English language, he became an avid reader of all publications written in the Hawaiian language. His most renowned book, *Mo'olelo Hawai'i* (*Hawaiian Antiquities*) was completed in 1839 and written entirely in Hawaiian. So within the span of eight years, from when he met Reverend Richards to his enrollment at Lahainaluna Seminary, he had already learned to read and write and even published a few smaller publications before starting on his book."

The missionaries founded Lahainaluna School, uphill from downtown Lahaina, in 1831. Ken Kimura, of the Lahaina Restoration Foundation, told me, "They had opened it as a seminary." The school's original purpose was to train Hawaiian men — David Malo was one of them — to be ministers. Kimura continues, "But within a year or so they started to invite the local kids up, and so they were running a regular school and a seminary in parallel. Overall, the missionaries accomplished a huge feat in getting the literacy rate up to a super high amount because the royalty was behind it." (By 1831, the missionaries' educational initiatives had the full support of Kaahumanu and King Kauikeaouli.) "The people wanted it," Kimura continues. "They had classrooms everywhere, classes in royalty's houses. It was regarded very highly to have an education."

Malo was born on the Big Island, near Kealakekua Bay, around 1793. His parents were habitués of the high chiefs' courts in Kamehameha's glory days, and so Malo grew up observing the rituals and customs of the nobility and learning the genealogies, dances, and chants of the Hawaiian oral tradition.

Malo's book *Hawaiian Antiquities,* a compendium of classical Hawaiian customs, beliefs, and vocabulary is intricate and wide-ranging. Malo details the impressive variety of fish hooks; burial practices; the codes and rituals of the ruling class; the names of a long list of gods, differentiating the god worshipped by robbers from the god worshipped by thieves; birth rituals; the kapu system; hula, sports, and games; chants and genealogies; how (and why) to build a house; fascinating and poetic delineations of time and phases of the moon — "the time when the plume of the sugar-cane began to unsheath itself" or the time when "the sharp points of the moon's horns are hidden." He records the words for sarcasm, intimidation, and bitterness. He reports that when choosing a tree from which to build a new canoe, if a priest has a dream about a naked man, then that tree is rotten and so the canoe should be built out of another tree.

If I were looking for one word to describe the Hawaiian people, "lucky" would not be it, but they were fortunate that the first real writer in the Hawaiian language happened to be one of the most knowledgeable keepers of the oral tradition. Malo was surely under the sway of the ministers. In *Hawaiian Antiquities* he proclaims, "The book that contains the word of Jehovah is of a value above every other treasure because it contains salvation for the soul." Still, by collecting and presenting the old chants and prayers, Malo made a tacit argument for their value and preservation during an era when missionaries were trying to eradicate the ancient rituals, especially the hula. He included the incantation recited when a chief was sick. He recorded, as well, the religious rites of fishermen as they prayed for a safe return from the sea: it was a call-

and-response affair, the priest calling out to the fishermen's god, "Save us from nightmare, from bad-luck-dreams, from omens of ill," the fishermen responding, "Defend us!" Even in the English translation it's clear that Malo takes pleasure in vocabulary, in the old rhythms of mystical songs.

One of Malo's most beautiful writings, a poem mourning the death of his friend Queen Kaahumanu in 1832, laments her passing as the end of conversation. Malo recalls their talks as treasure hunts. He has taken pen to paper as the ministers taught him but uses pen and paper to praise the power of speech, writing, "The voice is the staff that love leans upon."

Dwight Baldwin, one of the ABCFM's missionaries in Lahaina, said, "David Malo has, perhaps, the strongest mind of any man in the nation." After graduating from Lahainaluna Seminary, Malo stayed on to teach there, later becoming the first Hawaiian ordained to preach, as well as serving as Hawaii's first superintendent of schools.

Lahainaluna was the first public school in Hawaii (indeed, west of the Rockies), and it remains a thriving public high school to this day. The ringing school bell interrupts my conversation with Ken Kimura as he shows me around Hale Pa'i, the "house of printing," now a museum next to the school. Getting to the museum's front door involves weaving through groups of chatting, texting teenagers.

Inside the barnlike old building, Kimura says, "This is the print shop that the missionaries ran when the school first opened as a seminary. The school opened in 1831, and in 1834 they started printing. This was a support facility for creating materials for the school."

Pointing to the museum's Ramage printing press, he continues, "This is a working replica. We fire it up for school groups, and it is very similar to Benjamin Franklin's press, just a little bit smaller. It's still useable today. If we were to have a nuclear holocaust, I could still be printing newsletters on this thing."

Kimura notes, "The first paper money ever printed in Hawaii was printed in this shop. Only for use of the school, in exchange for the students' work. Unfortunately, Hale Pa'i is also known for the first counterfeit money ever printed in Hawaii, by the same people. They were expelled eventually."

He shows me a Temperance Map printed at Lahainaluna in 1843 after the social movement against alcohol arrived in Hawaii. It is a beautiful, if preachy, chart meant to steer the viewer away from the pitfalls of hooch. Kimura says, "The gist of it is that you start off on the Ocean of Animal Appetite. Hopefully you don't fall into the island of Poverty, Murder, Larceny, Brutality, or drown in Wine Lake, Beer Lake, Rum Lake, or Whiskey Lake. If you travel the high road in life, you might end up in the land of Industry, Improvement, Prosperity, Enjoyment. And eventually you might get over to the Ocean of Eternity."

"This is our claim to fame," Kimura says, drawing my attention to one of the display cases full of printed matter. "This is *Ka Lama Hawaii,* the first newspaper west of the Rockies."

Lorrin Andrews, the missionary who was Lahainaluna's first principal, reported to the ABCFM in 1834 of his intent to give the students "the idea of a newspaper — to show them how information of various kinds was circulated." *Ka Lama Hawaii,* Andrews wrote, "was designed as a channel through which the scholars might communicate their own opinions freely on any subject they chose."

Which sounds liberating, but in her history of Hawaiian newspapers, *Shaping History,* Helen Geracimos Chapin noted that the paper "spoke to the 'superiority' of

American culture, the Christian religion, and the Protestant work ethic. . . . By such 'truth in attractive form' were Hawaiian readers indoctrinated into the new culture."

Indoctrination was certainly the order of the day — Lahainaluna and its publications were supported by the ABCFM in Boston until 1848, when the Hawaiian Kingdom's government took over its administration. But the paper contained secular content as well. Chapin mentions the paper's publication of a series of woodblock illustrations of "forty four-footed beasts like the lion, camel, zebra, buffalo, and reindeer, all of which except for the dog and horse were unknown to the Hawaiians." It is a slight relief that the missionaries' educational discourse wasn't confined entirely to xenophobic, biblical diatribes. At least some of the information they imparted involved the simple presentation of new facts along the lines of *Guess what? Reindeer!*

The paper, distributed free of charge in Lahaina, only lasted about a year. "Then they had to focus back on their books," Kimura said. "They did a lot of textbook printing — history, math and science, all in Hawaiian."

Drawing my eye to a book on display written and published by Lahainaluna students in 1838, he says, "We have some original books here. This is of particular interest. It is called *Mo'olelo Hawaii*. It's the first history of Hawaii by Hawaiians in Hawaiian." David Malo and Samuel Kamakau, another important native historian, were among the students contributing to the book. Kimura points out that the book "continues to be printed today, in Honolulu, all in Hawaiian as a reference for immersion schools and Hawaiian studies."

A few days before Kimura and I spoke, about 150 Maui parents and other citizens staged a demonstration. Paia Elementary School, on the island's northern coast, had so many students sign up for its kindergarten Hawaiian-language immersion program that administrators planned to institute a lottery system to award enrollment by luck of the draw. The rally's organizers complained to the *Maui News* "that the lottery admission system denies children the right to Hawaiian language education and restricts the revitalization of Hawaiian language in communities."

After the overthrow of Queen Liliuokalani, Sanford Dole's regime passed a law in 1896 stating, "The English language shall be the medium and basis of instruction in all public and private schools." Hawaiian was not taught, and many schools prohibited speaking it, and students were punished for doing so well past statehood. Consequently, the language's usage dwindled and was on its way to becoming endangered until its revival during the Hawaiian Renaissance Movement of the 1960s and seventies.

As a minister and educator, David Malo contributed to Hawaii's Americanization by wielding all three weapons in Hiram Bingham's arsenal — "the school, the pulpit, and the press." But as Malo aged, and perhaps because he spent so much time pondering the old traditions in writing *Hawaiian Antiquities* or wading through Lahaina's crowds of seamen on leave, he became increasingly exasperated with the rising tide of haoles as the Hawaiians died and kept on dying. In a letter to native friends, he wrote:

If a big wave comes in, large and unfamiliar fishes will come from the dark ocean, and when they see the small fishes of the shallows they will eat them up. The white man's ships have arrived with clever men from the big countries. They know our people are few in number and our country is small, they will devour us.

Malo died in 1853. He wanted to be buried way up on a mountain above Lahainaluna School, on a slope where he hoped "no white man would ever build a house."

In 1969, as Hawaiians were beginning to revisit and revive the old traditions Malo wrote about and were learning to speak the Hawaiian language, Lahainaluna students founded a Hawaiiana Club as well as a chorus to study and perform Hawaiian-language songs and hula. Every April since 1970 Lahainaluna has celebrated David Malo Day. The Hawaiiana Club serves a poi supper in his honor, putting on a choral and hula pageant at sunset on the school grounds downhill from David Malo's lonesome grave. When Amy and Owen and I went, it seemed as though all of Lahaina showed up. Parents, alumni, and David Malo's descendants sat at long tables, eating poi and lau lau pork.

The students' performance was joyful and rigorous at the same time. It wasn't high school cute — it was impressive and intricate. Malo's translator, N. B. Emerson, also wrote a book about hula called *The Unwritten Literature of Hawaii* in which he pointed out, "We are wont to think of the old-time Hawaiians as light-hearted children of nature, given to spontaneous outbursts of song and dance as the mood seized them." On the contrary, Emerson continues, the hula required study and practice, "an organized effort, guarded by the traditions of a somber religion."

Wearing yellow leis, the Lahainaluna performers were all smiles but well rehearsed, dancing to Hawaiian songs and chants about the beauty of places such as Nuuanu and Hana and Kauai, with discipline and grace.

One of the students recited Malo's lines about the large and unfamiliar fishes eating up the small fishes, but the grim prophecy of his words wasn't in keeping with the optimism of the evening. The fish talk that summed up the pageant's hopeful air was the announcement that a graduating senior who won a David Malo Scholarship planned on majoring in marine biology at U of H in the fall. Slides were projected on a movie screen near the stage, portraits of historical queens like Kaahumanu and Liliuokalani, intermingled with photos of the students themselves. In the middle of a song called "O Kou Aloha," the students left the stage and searched for their mothers in the audience, bestowing leis upon the women. It was such a graceful, happy gesture that just about everyone teared up, including Owen.

He whispered, "If I could marry Hawaii, I would do it immediately."

The missionaries founded two elite schools in Honolulu in 1839 and 1841 — the Chiefs' Children's School, where the Hawaii State Capitol now stands, and Punahou, an academy for the children of the missionaries, a couple of miles from the mission complex. The final five Hawaiian monarchs attended the former school, Sanford Dole the latter. Dole, the only president of the Republic of Hawaii, was born on the Punahou campus. His father, Daniel, a missionary from Maine, was the school's first teacher.

Punahou was built on land Kaahumanu secured for Hiram and Sybil Bingham. The Binghams left for New England in 1840 due to Sybil's declining health. They never returned, though the night-blooming cereus bushes believed to have been planted by Sybil still grow on the property.

I met Laurel Douglass, an alumna of the Punahou School, Class of '58, at the Mission Houses Museum archives in Honolulu. A descendant of Amos Starr Cooke and Juliette Montague Cooke, the missionaries who ran the Chiefs' Children's School, Laurel was archive hopping that day, having spent the morning at the Bishop Museum. Within about a minute of the librarian from the Hawaiian Historical Society introducing us, she was rifling through a thick folder of papers to show me her morning's research. She had been reading the diary of Moses, a student at the school who was a grandson of Kamehameha I. She showed me an entry from August 22, 1843, when Moses noted, "When I awoke this morning then Mr. Cooke told that they had a nice baby." That baby, she said, was her great-something-grandmother Juliette.

At the time, that struck me as garden-variety genealogical homework, just a woman scouring historical records for mention of her ancestors. But that was before I got to know Laurel and learned about her special interest in Moses, an heir to the Hawaiian throne who died as a teenager during a measles epidemic. The way she talks about Moses and his schoolmates speaks to her interest in uncovering the truth about her forebears. Like any genealogical researcher, her blood pressure rises a bit when she sees Amos Cooke's name in print; in her case it is because she despises Cooke for beating the royal children with a whip.

Hawaiian history is more alive to her than

her own past. She lived on the mainland for a few years, dealing blackjack in Reno. "I was the worst blackjack dealer Harrah's ever turned out," she told me. "The pit boss told me that." It takes her a minute to remember what decade she moved to Nevada but when I ask her to walk me through the history of the Chiefs' Children's School, she gives me the precise date of Amos and Juliette Cooke's Connecticut wedding — "November 24, 1836."

"The two of them, through the ABCFM in Boston, they decided to apply for the Sandwich Islands Mission. They left Boston the very next month after they got married, December 1836, on the *Mary Frazier*. It was quite a large group of missionaries coming out here to the Sandwich Islands." She says that the Castles and the Wilcoxes were also on board, "three families that become very prominent over here. One of my brothers of the Cooke family marries one of the Wilcoxes five generations down the line. Everybody's going to be intermarrying each other, all these original missionaries. I'm the fifth generation here — all of us have been intermarried so many times. So we are all cousins, I guess.

"They arrived here in the islands April 9, 1837. By 1839, Mr. and Mrs. Cooke had been assigned to start a school, a private school in Honolulu, where the children of the chiefs will be taught." The missionaries reluctantly agreed to grant the king's request for a school for young aristocrats. Laurel notes, "King Kauikeaouli says, 'Okay, we'll take care of you, we'll respect your authority over the children, we'll give you some land, and we'll build a schoolhouse for you.' "

In his report to the ABCFM, Amos Cooke describes the meeting among the missionaries about whether or not to grant the king's request. He wrote, "The Mission voted, by a large majority, that we should relinquish our other labors and undertake it. Some did not vote because they did not like to have anything done to encourage the distinction between the children of Chiefs and common people." Cooke, speaking also for his wife, continued, "Under these circumstances we consented, unqualified as we were, to engage in this new school."

Cooke wasn't being modest. "The Cookes had no qualifications," Laurel points out. "Amos Cooke did not go to college at all."

Juliette wrote of her husband, "It has been rather heavy on Mr. Cooke having to teach subjects with which he is imperfectly acquainted, trigonometry, surveying, natural philosophy etc. He has been obliged to study nights in order to keep ahead of his class."

That the assembled missionaries would pawn off a couple with minimal book learning to teach the future monarchs speaks to their priorities. The mission's priority — first and last — was saving as many souls as possible. Daniel Dole, the colleague they entrusted with the education of their own children, was chosen to run Punahou because he lacked aptitude in the Hawaiian language and so was useless to teach and minister to Hawaiians, a great disappointment to Dole, considering that that's why he came to Hawaii in the first place.

Punahou became a world-class school and counts President Obama as an alumnus. When I got a tour of its impressive campus from Barb Morgan, a descendant of Hiram and Sybil Bingham, I felt like the president's grandfather when he took the tour with his grandson in the 1960s. Obama writes in his memoir *Dreams from My Father* that his grandfather whispered, " 'Hell, Bar, this isn't a school. This is heaven!' " I'm used to New York City public schools, where a school called the Secondary School for Journalism doesn't even have a school paper. When Morgan showed me Punahou's theater and its vast costume department, I asked her about drama classes. There are plenty of those, along with an entire course just on theater tech. Obama calls the place "an incubator for island elites." For that reason, it is seen as "the haole rich kid school," so much so that the coffee table book celebrating the school's 150th anniversary has an entire chapter titled "The Haole Rich Kids School," an attempt at confronting that reputation. At its founding, however, it was kind of a dump. The collection of the Mission Houses Archives includes a cranky letter Daniel Dole sent to Levi Chamberlain, complaining that the school's floors were so lopsided everything in the building rolls downhill.

As for the Chiefs' Children's School, Laurel says, "The five future monarchs of the kingdom are in that school as little children: Alexander Liholiho [Kamehameha IV], Lot Kamehameha [Kamehameha V], Lunalilo, David Kalakaua, and little Lydia [Liliuokalani]. The Cookes teach the children English, to write and communicate. The purpose of the school was to have the children submit and change to the American-Christian way, and give up their heathen, native ways. And the children resisted totally."

In a letter in 1839, Amos Cooke complains of Moses, "He is a very obstinate boy and I shall expect trouble with him."

"Moses became the troublesome one," Laurel says. "He was always sneaking out. Mr. Cooke starts going crazy, losing his temper, beating the children, catching them in bed with each other. You normally don't put boys and girls together in a boarding school with rooms all around each other, at the ages that they are — fourteen, fifteen, sixteen. You're asking for trouble. So Mr. Cooke sends off to Connecticut for a whip. He starts flogging these children. When you read his journal for September 22, 1845, Mr. Cooke hauls in the three Kamehameha brothers, who have been caught sneaking out the previous night, and Mr. Cooke brings one in and then the other and then the other, the three boys. He writes, 'And I struck Moses on the back, fifteen stripes, with the rawhide. Twenty stripes for Lot, who told such a story I struck him again.' He tells what he's done to them."

"That took place in 1845," Laurel says. "When I moved home to Maui [from Nevada], it was 1995, a hundred and fifty years later."

Upon returning home, she says she went into a flower shop in Maui and felt compelled to confess to the native Hawaiian lady working there, "I'm of the Cooke family."

Laurel remembers, "And she said, 'Yes, dear.'

"And I said, 'With the "e" at the end, you know the family?'

" 'Yes, dear.'

" 'Do you know they taught your royal children?'

" 'Yes, dear.'

" 'Do you know they also beat your royal children with a rawhide whip?'

" 'Yes, dear.'

" 'You do?' I could have fallen.

"And I say, 'Don't you think if your people ever put a curse on a family, they would put it on the family of the man who beat your royal children?'

"She looks at me — kind of looks up at me, she's smaller — and she puts her little hands across the glass counter, holds my two hands in hers, and says, right to my eyes, 'Yes, dear, forever. Hurry, tell the story.' "

I don't believe in curses, but I might if I had been through what Laurel has. When I ask her if there was anything in particular that made her want to start researching her family story, she answered without hesitating, "My son died. That was in Reno. He had just gone out for a bike ride. He was a good athlete, twenty-three years old. A kid ran a stop sign and hit him. So he was in the hospital with a head injury for thirteen days and then we had to turn the air off. I was forty-five when he died. And I just started reading, reading, reading, reading, reading. I had never read a thing about Hawaiian history. One of the books I read was *The Betrayal of Liliuokalani.* And when I read that, I don't know exactly how it affected me, but I couldn't stop."

Liliuokalani was the last alumna of the royal school to become a monarch before being ousted by alumni from Punahou School. "I was a studious girl," the queen wrote in her memoir. Regarding the Cookes, she recalls, "Our instructors were especially particular to teach us the proper use of the English language; but when I recall the instances in which we were sent hungry to bed, it seems to me that they failed to remember that we were growing children." Dinner, she says, was usually a slice of bread with molasses. It turns out the children weren't just sneaking out in search of fun. The queen writes that sometimes they snuck out to dig in the garden for roots or leaves they would cook on fires they made by rubbing sticks together.

Laurel says, "Amos Cooke said in his diary at the end of the time with the kids there, 'We have not accomplished our goal. Not one of the children has a changed heart.' "

If anything, the Cookes' harsh discipline and Dickensian mealtimes probably backfired in their goal of turning the royal children into grim New Englanders. David Kalakaua grew up to be the king nicknamed the "Merrie Monarch." When he toured the world in 1881, he wrote his sister a letter extolling the jollity of Vienna with its theaters, opera, races, and beer gardens. "Can it possibly be that these light hearted happy people are all going to H-ll?" Alluding to the missionaries back home, he continued, "But what a contrast to our miserable bigoted community. All sober and down in the mouth keeping a wrong Sabbath instead of a proper Sunday, the Pure are so pure that the impure should make the Sunday a day of mockery."

Though the Punahou students such as Sanford Dole and Lorrin A. Thurston (grandson of Asa and Lucy Thurston and Lorrin Andrews) are remembered for overthrowing Liliuokalani, in various ways the missionaries' children and the royal children all rebelled to some extent against the missionaries' disdain for worldly pursuits. When Sanford Dole went to Massachusetts to attend Williams College and then to Boston to study law, the letters to and from his parents back home in Hawaii, who hope he will join the ministry, include discussions of his increasingly alarming interests — dancing, card playing, theater, and "nude art." He writes that not only has he got a Catholic friend but he's been to a Catholic church to hear music and to a Unitarian church to teach a class. He disappoints his parents by informing them that not only will he not become a minister, he will become an attorney. In a subsequent letter he tries to address their fears that the practice of law is "dangerous to piety."

Perhaps irritated by scolding parental letters, Sanford writes from Boston in 1868, "I think the reason that the old missionaries have so little influence with the younger and wilder part of the people is because they thunder at them too much from the pulpit, and shun them too much in the affairs of daily life." Whatever disputes he and his Punahou mates will have with the alumni of the Chiefs' Children's School in the coming decades, on that point they would all agree.

In 1838, King Kauikeaouli hired the missionary William Richards to tutor him and other high chiefs at Lahaina in political science and act as a translator for the court. At which point Richards's employment by the ABCFM ended. That is worth remembering. Richards arrived in Hawaii in the second company of missionaries, a group whose instructions stressed that "it especially behooves a missionary to stand aloof from the private and transient interests of chiefs and rulers." Richards probably believed he was merely continuing his charge to be an all-around good influence on Hawaiians by acting New Englandy around them.

Richards was essentially Kauikeaouli's lackey, albeit a respected and influential one. One of his assignments from the king was to work with his old students at Lahainaluna, including David Malo, but especially a young Hawaiian noble named Boaz Mahune, to prepare briefs about constitutional law for government officials as the king geared up to refashion the absolute monarchy founded by his father, Kamehameha I, into a constitutional monarchy.

When scholar Keanu Sai and I were touring Honolulu's Judiciary Center, discussing Hawaii's legal history, he told me, "Kamehameha III [i.e., Kauikeaouli] did it of his own volition. And the chiefs were advising him. They were speaking about it." Sai brings up the fact that the Lahainaluna student Mahune was himself a chief: "So Boaz Mahune was tasked with drafting articles, presenting them to Kamehameha III and his chiefs, and then revising them. It wasn't some missionary telling them how to do it. This idea that the missionaries brought in constitutionalism, or forced it on the king, is outrageous."

The product of this collaboration, the Declaration of Rights of 1839, has been called the Hawaiian Magna Carta, alluding to the medieval English document proclaiming that the king was no longer above the law of the land. The Hawaiian declaration states, "It is by no means proper to enact laws for the protection of the rulers only." The declaration serves as the preamble to the Hawaiian Constitution issued the following year. It begins:

God hath made of one blood all nations of men to dwell on the earth, in unity and blessedness. God has also bestowed certain rights alike on all men and all chiefs, and all people of all lands. These are some of the rights which He has given alike to every man and every chief

217

of correct deportment; life, limb, liberty, freedom from oppression; the earnings of his hands and the productions of his mind, not however to those who act in violation of the laws.

The Constitution of 1840 establishes a House of Nobles comprised of chiefs and an elected legislature (to pass laws in concert with the nobles). Regarding legislation, "No law shall be enacted which is at variance with the word of the Lord Jehovah." The document also established a judiciary as well as governorships for each of the inhabited islands.

In 1839, the king also signed the Edict of Toleration. Kaahumanu had outlawed Catholicism at the request of the Protestant missionaries. Catholic missionaries were deported and Catholic converts were jailed. But after a French military frigate sailed to Honolulu, demanding reparations, Kauikeaouli legalized Catholicism much to the Protestants' dismay. Still, anti-Catholic traditions lingered among those in the missionaries' orbit. The missionaries were born into the anti-Catholic atmosphere of New England, a region settled by Pilgrims and Puritans who rejected what they saw as the Church of England's Catholic trappings. If the bright side of the Protestant Reformation is the revolution in literacy inspired by believers' need to read the Bible for themselves instead of receiving its teachings from the mouths of priests, the dark side of the movement was an often violent loathing of those priests, and the pope especially. The Geneva Bible the Puritan settlers brought with them to the New World identified the pope as the Whore of Babylon from the Book of Revelation. That New England missionaries imported this prejudice to Hawaii is evident in Isabella Bird's account of her travels to the islands in 1873 when, in a casual conversation with her native guide to Kilauea, the man "expressed a most orthodox horror of the Pope, who, he said, he knew from his Bible was the 'Beast!' "

Incidentally, I have met native Hawaiians who still have a bone to pick with the pope, but for a decidedly different reason than the missionaries. In fact, they identify the Catholic Church as the root cause of the coming of Catholic-hating Protestant missionaries to Hawaii, citing the papal bull *Inter caetera* of 1493, which charges Spain to Christianize the New World, as the founding document that bestowed moral justification on genocide and conquest. "The U.S. Manifest Destiny stems from that," one activist told me. The papal decree proposes "that barbarous nations be overthrown and brought to the faith itself." As this papal bull has never been rescinded, some Hawaiians have joined indigenous peoples internationally in organizing protests in which they gather in front of Catholic churches to burn copies of the decree.

Fearing further foreign intervention, in 1842 King Kauikeaouli dispatched his secretary, a Lahainaluna-educated member of the House of Nobles named Timothy Haalilio to travel to the United States and Europe with William Richards to establish formal diplomatic relations with the U.S., England, and France. Arriving in Washington in December, the diplomats were informed by Secretary of State Daniel Webster that President John Tyler deemed a formal treaty unnecessary. (England and France issued a joint declaration of Hawaiian independence a few months later.) However, the Hawaiian representatives did receive a letter from Webster that historian Ralph Kuykendall calls "the document that is commonly cited as the first formal recognition of the independence of the Hawaiian kingdom."

Webster, acknowledging that most of the

ship traffic passing through Hawaii was American, wrote, "The United States, therefore, are more interested in the fate of the islands, and of their Government, than any other nation can be." Webster continued, "The Government of the Sandwich Islands ought to be respected; that no power ought either to take possession of the islands as a conquest, or for the purpose of colonization." President Tyler then forwarded Webster's letter to Congress along with a message asserting that the United States would be justified "should events hereafter arise, to require it, in making a decided remonstrance against the adoption of an opposite policy by any other power." Which hints at military intervention should another country invade Hawaii.

Kuykendall points out that after Tyler's message was read in the House of Representatives, on December 31, an opportunistic congressman connected the recent history of Hawaii to "the unsettled Oregon question." That question — whether the Oregon Territory was to be American or British — was threatening to lead to war and wouldn't be settled until 1846, when the current Canadian border was drawn.

In other words, the first time the United States government acknowledged Hawaiian independence, the islands were nevertheless unwittingly roped into a Capitol Hill debate about American expansionism.

On January 24, 1843, a few weeks after Congress received President Tyler's message recognizing Hawaiian independence, the House Committee on Foreign Affairs, chaired by John Quincy Adams, drew hope for an American future in Oregon from the accomplishments of the missionaries in Hawaii who brought the islands "from the lowest debasement of idolatry . . . to the fold of civilization by a written language and constitution." The committee's point was to praise the civilizing effects of American boots on the ground. On second thought, not boots — New England ladies' shoes.

Although for Washington politicians the connection between Oregon and Hawaii was metaphorical in 1843, Hawaiians had been trading busily with the Hudson's Bay Company's Oregon outpost for years. Kuykendall posits that Oregon "lumber was shipped to the islands as early as 1829, and salmon as early as 1830." The boom years of whaling only intensified the economy and, as Kuykendall claims, "It is probably safe to say that Honolulu and other growing Hawaiian towns of the middle of the [nineteenth] century were built very largely with lumber brought from the Columbia River and Puget Sound."

In May of 1843, the first big wagon train of nearly a thousand settlers hit the Oregon Trail. That June, President Tyler submitted his treaty for the annexation of Texas to the Senate, where it failed to pass. Tyler's successor, James K. Polk, annexed Texas through a joint resolution two years later in December of 1845, signing the treaty for Oregon six months after that. New York writer John L. O'Sullivan called these acquisitions America's "manifest destiny."

Oregon, O'Sullivan opined in the *New York Morning News,* belonged to the United States because it was "our manifest destiny to overspread and to possess the whole of the continent which Providence has given us." His generation, he predicts, will preside over "a noble young empire in the Pacific."

Even though originally the concept of Manifest Destiny, as stated by O'Sullivan, involved the divine right of the United States to occupy the North American continent from sea to sea, bold and grabby visionaries began to think bigger. As the joint resolution to annex Texas was being considered in 1845, Congressman John Wentworth of Illinois imagined the future delight of hearing the Speaker of the House recognizing "the gentleman from Texas" and "the gentleman from Oregon." But Wentworth pined for yet more gentlemen: "the gentleman from Nova Scotia, the gentleman from Canada, the gentleman from Cuba, the gentleman from Mexico, aye, even the gentleman from Patagonia."

In 1849, French marines attacked the fort at Honolulu to protest unfair treatment of Catholics and excessive duties on French liquors. The sailors retreated but the incident prompted the Hawaiian government to dispatch diplomats abroad to seek treaties with foreign powers to shore up support for Hawaiian independence. The United States signed a formal treaty with Hawaii that year, proclaiming, "There shall be perpetual peace and amity between the United States and the King of the Hawaiian Islands, his heirs and his successors."

In addition to the United States, Britain, and France, Hawaii would eventually enjoy diplomatic relations with a number of countries, including Denmark, Sweden, Belgium, Italy, Russia, Germany, Portugal, Samoa, and Japan.

The adoption of the Hawaiian Constitution of 1840 and the establishment of diplomatic relations abroad speak to the haoles' influence on the Hawaiian government, but they also reflect King Kauikeaouli's active leadership in Westernizing his kingdom and asserting Hawaiian sovereignty before the rest of the world.

Kauikeaouli's most radical reform by far was the so-called Great Mahele, the land division of 1848. That year, as Hawaii's official new friends the French and the Danes revolted against their monarchs, as Marx and Engels published their class-warfare classic *The Communist Manifesto,* the king of Hawaii was voluntarily giving up much of the land he controlled just as he had voluntarily given up some of his power by commissioning a constitution.

Hawaiian land, previously controlled entirely by the king, was divided among the king, the government, the chiefs, and the commoners. Which sounds straightforward enough, though down the road many a Honolulu attorney will log billable hours untangling the weird aftereffects of what happens to crown lands after a monarchy has been overthrown.

Back in 1835, a Bostonian named William Hooper arrived in Koloa, on the island of Kauai, with permission from Kamehameha III to start the first sugar plantation in the Sandwich Islands. On the one-year anniversary of the plantation's founding, Hooper confided in his diary that the introduction of wage labor and for-profit agriculture in Hawaii would "serve as an entering wedge" that would "upset the whole system."

Hawaiians' role in providing food for the surge of American settlers to Oregon and California in the 1840s contributed to increasingly prosperous planters lobbying the king to privatize the land. In an 1846 letter, the missionary Richard Armstrong wrote, "A brisk trade is opening with Oregon and California. . . . The sugar and molasses of the islands will be in demand in these territories and they will bring lumber, flour, salmon, etc. in exchange." After the California gold rush of 1849, Armstrong reported, "Every bean, onion, potato or squash that we have to spare is at once snatched away to California to feed the hungry there."

As Hawaiian planters expanded their operations, it was only natural for them to want to secure their fields from the whims of chiefs or the king. They wanted ownership, and they wanted paperwork proving ownership.

The Hawaiian government did not simply chop up maps of the islands and pass out deeds to commoners and chiefs. A Land Commission ruled on claims. Many commoners did not receive the land set aside for them because in order for a commoner to receive the deed to his allotted land, he had to petition the Land Commission. As Jon M. Van Dyke writes in his book *Who Owns the Crown Lands of Hawai'i?*:

The factors frequently mentioned for the low number of land awards include the unfamiliarity of the [commoners] with the concept of private property, the failure to educate them about the changes and the steps they needed to take to claim property, the difficulty in filing and providing claims (which required a survey for a fee that many did not have), the short period of time allowed to file and prove claims, which was particularly burdensome on the natives living in the country . . . fraud, conflicts of interest, favoritism, delays in processing claims, and the interference of some [chiefs] who sought to discourage such claims.

Because the idea of private property was so new and the bureaucracy involved was so labyrinthine, David Malo, writes John H.

Chambers, "[was] opposed to allowing land to be sold to foreigners and wanted a ten-year moratorium during which to educate native Hawaiians about land ownership." Malo's suggestion was ignored.

Van Dyke concludes that "out of the 1,523,000 acres given to the Government by Kauikeaouli for his people, only 28,658 acres, or less than 1 percent of Hawaii's land area" went to the commoners.

Researching land records on Oahu for his book *Kahana: How the Land Was Lost,* Robert Stauffer found that in cases where commoners petitioned for land they and their ancestors had been cultivating for generations, their "homesteads were fully developed and productive and came with water rights through existing irrigation systems." He argues that though the commoners occupied only a wee fraction of land, it was some of Hawaii's best land, assessing the value of the commoners' homesteads at "about $2.7 billion (in 2000 dollars), or almost half of all the land values."

Stauffer blames an 1874 law privatizing mortgage foreclosures for commoners' biggest land losses, not the initial Mahele rulings. Still, per the Kuleana Act of 1850, the government could sell unclaimed land for fee simple to anyone, including foreigners.

By May of that year alone, according to Van Dyke, "the Government had sold about 2,700 parcels of government land on all the islands. . . . Most of the individual purchasers were Hawaiians, but foreigners acquired almost two-thirds of the total land area."

In the end, due to unclaimed lands, mortgage foreclosures, gifts, or purchases of crown lands and garden-variety real estate sales and leases, haoles controlled about ninety percent of the land by 1890. Privatizing property ultimately resulted in the commoners, the "eyes of the land," being left with little ground to watch over.

As the U.S. Civil War denied the North access to Louisiana sugar, Hawaiian planters stepped into the breach. Cane fields soon replaced taro patches.

For that reason, the popular refrain is that haoles "stole" the land. "Cry for the land that was taken away," sang Israel Kamakawiwoʻole in his song "Hawaii '78." However, nearly all of these transactions, even the fishiest, were legal. I'm not sugarcoating. To me, confronting the practical and moral limits of the law is far more disturbing than what *The Communist Manifesto* called mere "naked self-interest." Expecting capitalists to refrain from gobbling up the earth is like blaming Pac-Man for gulping down pac-dots — to them, that's what land is for. Which is kind of the reason the manifesto called for abolishing private land ownership the very year Hawaii started privatizing land ownership. (Not that implementing the Marxist vision worked out so well in the long run either.)

The commie-quoting sucker in me wonders what happened to government regulation. The answer to that goes back to Kauikeaouli's good intentions. The king had honorable motives in giving commoners land and establishing a constitution limiting his own powers. Yet those two decisions were deciding factors in the increase of haole control over the government and the land.

Take, for instance, the judiciary established by the Constitution of 1840. Great idea. Problem was, no lawyers. (Insert joke here.) William Little Lee, a New Yorker who graduated from Harvard Law, was sailing to Oregon to start a new life in 1846 when ship repairs forced a stopover in Honolulu and he got talked into sticking around to become the first justice of the Hawaii Supreme Court. The other lawyer in town, John Riccord, had already become the kingdom's attorney general.

When Keanu Sai and I were standing next

to an oil portrait of Lee in the Judiciary History Center, he said of Lee and Riccord, "They weren't Puritans, they were lawyers. When they came, they were approached by the Hawaiian government to join the government, because what Hawaii needed to do, for its own self-protection, was to utilize people's experience in areas of constitutional systems of government, because Hawaii didn't have that experience. It came from an absolute rule, a feudal, aristocratic rule. That was the history of Hawaii."

Sai, nodding at the portrait of Lee, said, "He gets a bum rap. See, a lot of people say, 'If he's haole, he's bad.' That's wrong, that's very wrong. He was good. Very good. When he came, Hawaii was six years into being a constitutional monarchy. And he was a proponent of securing the people's rights to the land and ensuring the monarch is limited, and held to be limited, in a constitutional form of government without being overbearing."

Thus, in order to build his new government it was only logical that Kauikeaouli would consult and include some of the best-educated people at hand. So whites, many of them ex-missionaries, were incorporated into the constitutional government from the beginning. Lorrin Andrews, for example, the former principal of Lahainaluna School, joined the Hawaiian Supreme Court as an associate justice after he resigned from his missionary post in protest of the ABCFM's acceptance of donations from slave states.

To work for the government, the foreigners stopped being foreigners, renouncing their American citizenship to become subjects of the kingdom. But that did not mean they suddenly lost their American prejudices and ideals, including a fundamental belief in the morality of private property, free enterprise, and agriculture-as-culture. They governed accordingly.

Robert Stauffer, the scholar who cites an 1874 mortgage foreclosure law for separating most commoners from their homesteads, remarks that the law was introduced by a haole to a legislature "presided over by the leading banker of the day, an American, who incidentally would be expecting increases in both his own business and his profits through an opening of a market for these lands." And if that law's constitutionality had been challenged, Stauffer notes, it would have been decided by an all-white court. He summarizes that in the half century before the overthrow of 1893, "wherein the bulk of land was lost, 94 percent of Supreme Court justices were Haole, as were 82 percent of the extremely powerful executive cabinet members and a great many legislative leaders."

The monarchs, beginning with Kauikeaouli, welcomed these unfamiliar fishes into the government. If it is understandable that native Hawaiians wanted to hold on to some of their ancient traditions, it is also understandable that naturalized Hawaiians of New England stock held on to some of their ancestral traditions, such as the sanctity of private property (and, eventually, revolting against monarchs).

Oni v. Meek, a case that came before Hawaii's Supreme Court in 1858, perfectly illustrates the two worldviews in conflict during that transitional age. A native Hawaiian named Oni let his grazing horses stray outside of the boundaries of his land onto property leased by a Massachusetts-born rancher named John Meek. In the ancient Hawaiian land system, commoners were assigned land to farm by their landlord chief but were generally permitted grazing rights elsewhere in that chief's purview.

Finder's keepers, thought Meek, who seized Oni's horses. A Honolulu police court ruled that Meek should return Oni's horses. When Meek appealed to the Hawaii Supreme Court, Oni asserted the grazing customs of old. The all-white court ruled in favor of Meek, claiming that Oni "has no pretense for claiming a right of pasturage by custom." Their decision made clear that Oni's old way of doing things had become "so unreasonable, so uncertain, and so repugnant to the spirit of the present laws, that it ought not to be sustained by judicial authority."

When I read that, I thought the decision might have been legally justified but that the word "repugnant" stuck out as a tad vindictive, and thus culturally motivated. "Repugnant" has a snobby subtext, which makes sense, considering its French origin. But my attorney friend Bill told me lawyers throw around the word "repugnant" all the time, that it's everyday legalese. He said, "It is a word we would use, for example, in saying that a certain action is repugnant to the intent of a statute." Then he called me a "legal realist" for factoring human foibles and cultural biases into the making and interpretation of laws.

Coincidentally, as I was reading about the Hawaii Supreme Court's ruling on *Oni v. Meek,* the confirmation hearings for U.S. Supreme Court nominee Sonia Sotomayor were on TV. Senators — particularly Senator Jeff Sessions, a white male representing

Alabama — were grilling her about a speech she made referring to herself as a "wise Latina woman," in which she hinted at possessing different, if not superior, insights from those of her white male colleagues. Sotomayor is of Puerto Rican descent, and some of the senators worried that she was biased in favor of her own gender and ethnicity. She replied that judges aren't "robots." Still, she maintained, "We have to recognize feelings and put them aside," adding, "In every case where I have identified a sympathy, I have articulated it and explained to the litigant that the law requires a different result."

Naturally, when I came across that exchange, the first thing I thought of was the Kepaniwai Heritage Gardens. This is a lovely little park in Maui next to Iao Valley State Park, site of Kamehameha the Great's "Damming of the Waters" battle. Built in 1952, Kepaniwai honors the architecture of Maui's original inhabitants and immigrants, featuring a traditional Hawaiian grass house, a Portuguese oven, a Filipino hut, a Japanese teahouse, a Chinese pagoda, a Korean gate, and a New England missionary's house. When my sister saw it, she said, "Come over to my house!" *Come Over to My House* was one of our favorite books as kids. Written by "Theo. LeSieg," aka Theodor Geisel, aka Dr. Seuss, the book featured cheerful drawings of igloos, stilt houses, and gondolas to illustrate the way of life of kids around the world, leading to the conclusion, "They're all, all alike when a friend asks you in."

Amid the Buddhist silhouettes in the Kepaniwai Gardens, the puritanical Massachusetts saltbox looks as exotic — as ethnic — as the pagoda. So when I saw a white guy from Alabama ask a New York Puerto Rican if her heritage warped her judgment, I thought of that saltbox, and couldn't help but laugh.

When the Hawaiian government made it legal for foreigners to own land in 1850, the end of the American Revolutionary War was only sixty-seven years in the past. And one of the issues the revolutionaries fought over was the sanctity of private property. The British government forcing colonists to house its soldiers in their homes and businesses was one of the colonists' major grievances; they brought it up in the Declaration of Independence and later ratified the Third Amendment to guarantee that a homeowner is not required to quarter government troops without consent. To the Don't-Tread-On-Me generation and their offspring a property line is a line in the sand.

I'm not trying to excuse the racial imbalance of land ownership in Hawaii — that's always going to be upsetting. I'm simply pointing out that to the haoles the acquisition of property had a deeper meaning than simple greed. To them, cultivating land was damn near theological. When the Reverend John Cotton preached his farewell sermon to the Massachusetts Bay colonists in 1630, he told his fellow Puritans, "In a vacant soil, he that taketh possession of it, and bestoweth culture and husbandry upon it, his right it is." Cotton backed up this statement, quoting Genesis: "Multiply, and replenish the earth, and subdue it." Recall that when Timothy Dwight preached the founding sermon at Andover Theological Seminary, he lauded Cotton's generation of Puritans because they "converted *New-England* from a desert into a garden." And he meant that both spiritually and literally.

In Hawaii, the racial resentment over haoles' post-1850 land ownership is, like Kilauea, an active volcano. One man I met on Oahu, who asked me not to use his name, told me about attending a series of public discussions in 2002 called the "Sovereignty Sessions." This fellow is white and was born and raised in Honolulu. He said that these meetings, devoted to discussing the issue of Hawaiian independence, "featured about ten 'Hawaiians' — people of Hawaiian ancestry, but very few, if any, with more than one-quarter blood quantum — speaking with ten or so non-Hawaiians about the issue of sovereignty and its implications for Hawaii. Before each of the three three-hour sessions, we would serve ourselves from a provided buffet dinner and we would give our thanks in prayer to Jesus, or the Christian God, which I immediately found curious. After eating, we would discuss the issues surrounding sovereignty as the two moderators, one 'Hawaiian' and one non-Hawaiian, asked questions and attempted to separate emotion from fact. I remember the first meeting being very polite, and as a result not very productive or informative. In the second meeting, after the prayer and the eating, the gloves came off. In my opinion, the 'Hawaiians' were very aggressive, throwing around words like 'genocide' with respect to the decline of the Hawaiian culture, and 'theft' in regards to the issue of land, and how the creation of a native Hawaiian government comprised only by people who had Hawaiian blood was the only way to possibly redress the wrongs perpetrated onto them. My most distinct memory is of a non-Hawaiian gentleman asking, more or less, 'You act like the missionaries were purely evil and provided nothing of value to the Hawaiian people, but didn't they give you a written language that has enabled the Hawaiian language to persist to this very day? Didn't they give you your God? Several of you have referenced God in decrying what the missionaries supposedly did — but would you rather have your land or God? I'm sure you would all say you want both, but that's simply not possible and not the case, so which is it?' There was silence as people digested that stark choice. I think the conversation shifted to whether the missionaries did actually 'steal' the land, which of course depends on your interpretation."

Hawaiian words remind me of how a friend once described looking at the vast list of departing flights at Hong Kong International Airport. He said he liked the feeling of standing before the enumeration of destination cities, knowing he could go in so many different directions. A Hawaiian word can have so many meanings and associations that each noun becomes a portal into stories and beliefs, like how the word for wealth, *waiwai,* is just the word for water spoken twice. I started asking Hawaiians what words meant even when I knew the answer because I became addicted to seeing them crinkle their brows into Talmudic squints as they tried to call forth a word's nuances.

The hypothetical dilemma reportedly presented by that man during the sovereignty discussions — land or God — is folded into the word *palapala*. In the definitive *Hawaiian Dictionary,* compiled by Mary Kawena Pukui and Samuel H. Elbert, *palapala* is defined as "Document of any kind, bill, deed, warrant, certificate, policy, letter, tract, writ, diploma, manuscript; writing of any kind, literature; printing on tapa or paper; formerly the Scriptures or learning in general; to write, send a written message." Just as the word *haole* describes both a missionary and the sailors shooting a cannon at the missionary's house, *palapala* encapsulates what Westerners brought with them to Hawaii, from literature and diplomas to bills and deeds.

In 1840, the artist Alfred Agate drew a missionary who came to offer one kind of *palapala* — learning and God — but would stay to enjoy the other kind — a deed to Hawaiian land. In the picture, William P. Alexander, who sailed to Hawaii from New Bedford with the ABCFM's fifth company of missionaries, preaches to natives seated on the ground in a grove of kukui trees near a beach on Kauai.

Agate's engraving appears in the published account of the naval expedition the U.S. Congress authorized to circumnavigate the globe in 1838, the year Queen Liliuokalani was born. The United States South Seas Exploring Expedition, known as the "Ex.Ex.," was America's attempt at a scholarly/commercial/military voyage for the whaling age in the manner of Cook and La Pérouse. Lieutenant Charles Wilkes and the six ships under his command were to map, survey, document, and collect scientific specimens. (The specimens they brought home ended up being the basis of the Smithsonian's collections.) As Nathaniel Philbrick writes in *Sea of Glory,* "the Expedition logged 87,000 miles, surveyed 280 Pacific islands, and created 180 charts — some of which were still being used as late as World War II."

Philbrick continues, "The Expedition also mapped 800 miles of coastline in the Pacific Northwest." If the kukui tree that dwarfs William Alexander in Agate's portrait of the missionary is impressive, it's nothing compared to an old-growth pine in an Oregon forest that Agate depicts in a scene with a couple of sailors who are trying to measure it, a tree of such monstrous height and girth that a Congress already salivating for Oregon would no doubt drool when they saw it.

Nevertheless, those kukui trees Agate drew on the expedition's stopover in Kauai, wrote Lieutenant Wilkes, "are large and form a delightful shade." The kukui is what is known as a "canoe plant." The ancient Polynesian voyagers who settled Hawaii brought the kukui with them in their canoes, canoes that were waterproofed with the oil of the kukui nut. Hawaiians made dye to decorate tapa cloth out of kukui bark, strung together kukui nuts to make leis for the chiefs, and used oil from the nuts to seal their surfboards and light their lamps and torches. It's no wonder the kukui is now the Hawaii state tree.

Wilkes wrote of Alexander's sermon in the kukui grove, "There are few places in the open air so well calculated to hold divine service in, and it is well fitted to create feelings of religion."

Later, Alexander will run the Lahainaluna School. Then he will go on to own a sugar plantation. His son Samuel will be one of the founders of Alexander & Baldwin, one of the "Big Five" corporations, Noenoe

Silva writes, "that controlled Hawaii's economy for many decades." (In fact, today, the mill on Maui operated by an Alexander & Baldwin subsidiary is the last operating sugar mill in the Hawaiian Islands.)

Silva describes the increasingly blurry line between the missionaries' mandate to convert the natives and their participation in the land's conversion from subsistence crops to commercial agriculture. She cites William P. Alexander's 1860 report to the ABCFM: "We have hundreds of acres of fertile soil that might be easily irrigated by our perennial streams that burst forth from our mountain glens, yet we produce almost nothing but [taro]: whereas we ought to produce and export a thousand tons of sugar annually." Silva points out that nowadays, taro, the Hawaiians' staple food for centuries is "scarce and expensive as a result of the change to a cash economy based on sugar, pineapple, and tourism."

Alexander's capitalist comment that the land was wasted on taro when they could have been raking it in with cane, while decidedly un-Hawaiian, should probably be considered in light of the letter the Sandwich Islands Mission received from ABCFM headquarters in 1849 advising the missionaries to begin the process of weaning themselves, their schools, and their churches from the board's financial support. The board encouraged the ministers who wanted to stay in Hawaii to seek employment and become subjects of the kingdom. The board offered grants to ease the transition but counseled the missionaries to negotiate with the government to take over support of schools and to step up the training of native preachers to take over the soon-to-be self-supporting churches. So it makes sense that Alexander and his colleagues would seek agricultural, commercial, and political opportunities.

In the case of another future Big Five company, Castle & Cooke, the business had its very origins in the mission's depository of supplies: Amos Starr Cooke left the Chiefs' Children's School in 1849, joining his former shipmate William Castle to assume the duties of the late Levi Chamberlain. Two years later the two opened the Honolulu store that would grow into a conglomerate by purveying the same sort of sundries Chamberlain used to forward to the various mission stations.

The ABCFM closed the Sandwich Islands Mission in 1863 and the missionaries and their children who stuck around had to earn a living. Given that the American Civil War was ratcheting up the demand for Hawaiian sugar, it's not surprising that some of the godly families shifted their attention away from heaven and toward the red dirt.

In the decades between the Great Mahele of 1848 and the overthrow of the monarchy in 1893, the two most crucial issues in Hawaii were sugar and death.

"With the coming of strangers," wrote the Lahainaluna graduate Samuel Kamakau, "there came contagious diseases which destroyed the native sons of the land."

In their article on the epidemics of 1848–49 for the *Hawaiian Journal of History,* Robert C. Schmitt and Eleanor C. Nordyke estimate that ten thousand people (one tenth of the population) died in the islands in those two years alone. They attribute the alarming uptick in deaths from measles, whooping cough, dysentery, influenza, and diarrhea to the amplified ship traffic between Hawaii and the West Coast brought on by the California gold rush. They point out:

Before the late 1840s, most ships visiting Hawai'i sailed from East Coast ports, and reached the Islands by a long, laborious voyage around South America.

Any sick seamen were either dead or recovered by the time they sighted Diamond Head. Now they sailed directly from San Francisco in perhaps two weeks or less, fully capable of spreading the baleful diseases they had so recently picked up.

Describing a subsequent epidemic that may have killed as many as five thousand inhabitants of Oahu in 1853, Kamakau recalled, "The smallpox came, and dead bodies lay stacked like kindling wood, red as singed hogs." In Honolulu, "the disease broke out like a volcanic eruption." And then:

The dead fell like dried kukui twigs tossed down by the wind. Day by day from morning till night horse-drawn carts went about from street to street of the town, and the dead were stacked up like a load of wood, some in coffins, but most of them just piled in, wrapped in cloth with heads and legs sticking out.

Among the high chiefs, the nineteenth-century death rate was as high as the birth rate was low. In her memoir, Queen Liliuokalani describes that during the measles epidemic of 1848, three of her childhood peers, including Kamehameha I's grandson

Moses, "were buried on the same day, the coffin of the last-named resting on that of the others."

Kamehameha the Great, the founder of the Hawaiian Kingdom, was the first and last monarch to father heirs who survived childhood to rule. When the thirty-year reign of Kamehameha III ended with his possibly alcohol-related death in 1854, his only son was the product of an extramarital affair and thus not eligible for the throne. So his nephew was sworn in as Kamehameha IV; he then died of asthma at twenty-nine.

Kamehameha V signed "An Act to Prevent the Spread of Leprosy" into law in 1865. That year, with nearly three thousand reported cases of what is now called Hansen's disease, a hospital was built on Oahu. The following year, the first exiles were sent to a permanent, segregated settlement on Molokai's Kalaupapa Peninsula, an isolated sliver of land cut off from the rest of the island by the steepest sea cliffs on earth. "A prison fortified by nature," Robert Louis Stevenson called it after spending a week there in 1889. Exile was permanent and patients were at times removed from their homes by force. Legally mandated segregation remained Hawaiian law until 1969, which was twenty-three years after the arrival of a cure. Over the course of the century it existed, the Molokai colony confined an estimated eight thousand patients. At the time of the 1893 overthrow, Kalaupapa had more than a thousand residents. (One of Sanford Dole's early tasks as president was to declare martial law on Kauai to facilitate a manhunt for a Hawaiian known as Koolau who was afflicted with Hansen's disease. Koolau had shot and killed the deputy sheriff who tried to apprehend him for the purpose of shipping him to Molokai. Koolau escaped with his wife, Piilani, and their son to hide in Kauai's remote cliffs and valleys for three years. While on the lam in the backwoods, the son took ill. Then Koolau and his wife buried the little boy. Then Koolau died and his wife buried him. Then she emerged from the wilderness alone. As she hiked down, she later recalled, "The mountains and forests were lonely. Only the brush of the breeze on my cheeks and the rustle of the leaves on the trees were my travelling companions, besides my recollections.")

Kamehameha V, the last of Kamehameha the Great's direct descendants to rule, died in 1872; suffering from an abscess, a kidney disorder, and a cold, the king remarked, "It is hard to die on my birthday." His cousin and successor, William Charles Lunalilo, ended his short reign spitting up blood; when he died of tuberculosis, his reign had lasted thirteen months.

When David Kalakaua became king in 1874, his motto was "Ho'oulu A Ho'ola Lahui" — Increase the Race. In fact, the native Hawaiian population decreased by 15,000 during his reign. By 1890, there were only about 40,000 natives of pure or part Hawaiian blood — compared to a minimum of 300,000 on Captain Cook's arrival.

Kalakaua, like his short-lived predecessor Lunalilo, was elected king. "Can you imagine?" a Honolulu cab driver asked me as we were chatting about Hawaiian history on the way to the airport. A transplant from Illinois, he said, "Who ever heard of electing a king?"

Reading descriptions of Kalakaua as a "king-elect" does look peculiar to my American eyes, but the previous two monarchs had died without heirs and without naming successors. Hence the legislature's election of two kings, a development that manages to combine the worst drawbacks of democracy and monarchy — the hostility of opposing parties and the unfair limitations of aristocratic bloodlines. (Naturally, only the high chiefs were eligible candidates, narrowing the options to alumni of the Chiefs' Children's School.)

In Kalakaua's case, his opponent was his former schoolmate the dowager Queen Emma, the widow of Kamehameha IV. Many Hawaiians considered Emma to be of higher rank than Kalakaua because she was more closely related to the Kamehameha line; not only had she married the grandson of Kamehameha the Great, but the first monarch was her great-great-uncle and she was also a cousin of his sacred wife, Keopuolani. Kalakaua's ancestors had been Kamehameha's generals; farther back, they shared some remote grandfather. Which sounds pretty semantical to me, but genealogy was — and is — serious business to Hawaiians.

Emma's faction was pro-British, believing in fostering deeper ties to Great Britain for its longstanding friendship and support for Hawaiian independence. In fact, the British government had been quick to restore Hawaiian sovereignty when one of its rogue naval officers claimed the islands for the British crown without authorization for a few months in 1843. (Modern Hawaiian independence activists still celebrate Sovereignty Day, the anniversary of the date the Brits apologized for the mix-up and restored Kamehameha III to full power, by holding protests against what they see as the ongoing American occupation.) The Anglophile Emma saw shoring up the islands' cordial relationship with the United Kingdom as a way of staving off annexation by the United States. Even after she lost the election to Kalakaua, she wrote the British commissioner to Hawaii, intent on sussing out Britain's position on accepting Hawaii as its protectorate because, as she wrote, "I consider that America is now our open enemy." She added, "The Native Hawaiians are one with me in the love of our country, and determined not to let Hawaii become a part of the United States of America." The British diplomat replied in the negative, pointing out that if Britain made such a move, it could lead to war with the U.S.

Kalakaua's side was (more or less) pro-American, in that they were devoted to nurturing economic ties with the United States, focusing on the sugar trade. Obviously, he won the support of the planters. Kalakaua saw economic prosperity as a way of sustaining Hawaiian independence, and the United States was Hawaii's largest market by far.

When Emma's supporters learned that Kalakaua had won the election with thirty-nine votes (to her nine), they rioted. They rushed the courthouse and started ripping it up, breaking windows and furniture, clubbing legislators with shards of chairs and tossing one of them out a second-story window. The architect of the later overthrow, Lorrin Thurston, at the time a Punahou student who ditched class to witness the hubbub, recalled: "A rain of books, papers, chairs, tables, and other furniture poured from the doors and windows of the courthouse. . . . Some members of the Legislature crawled from the windows and hung on the outside of the building by their hands. The mob stamped on their fingers, so that they fell into the street below."

Kalakaua, the king-elect — that does look weird — sent messages to the British and American warships that were in the harbor requesting that they dispatch troops to help restore order. One eyewitness at the courthouse recalled that the American troops arrived first but that the rioters met the British reinforcements "with cheers" because the mob, like its candidate, was pro-British. They were disappointed when the Brits helped the Americans quiet things down.

Sanford Dole was among the witnesses of

the scuffle and he and his brother pitched in to help calm the mob. Nineteen years later, when Dole and his coconspirators overthrew Kalakaua's sister, Liliuokalani, they colluded with the United States Minister to Hawaii to land American troops from the USS *Boston,* then anchored in the harbor, to provide military backup to the haoles. In *Hawaii's Story by Hawaii's Queen,* Liliuokalani rejects the notion that calling on foreign troops to put down the rioting Emmaites established a dangerous precedent repeated in 1893 when she was ripped from the throne. "When armed forces were landed [in 1874]," she wrote, "it was to sustain and protect the constitutional government at a mere momentary emergency from a disloyal mob." The constitutional government of 1893, she pointed out, *"absolutely protested"* the American Marines' arrival on shore.

Her interpretation is technically correct — no question. There's a big difference between asking foreign troops' help in getting a few sore losers to stop throwing people out of windows and using foreign troops to facilitate a coup d'état. Still, if Kalakaua's decision did not set a legal precedent, it did set a precedent in the wielding of power. Sanford Dole and his cronies had witnessed foreign troops intervening at government buildings in Honolulu during a politically twitchy transition. Regardless of the constitutional principle involved, foreign troops intervening at Hawaiian government buildings during twitchy transitions became thinkable.

Hawaiian historian Jonathan Osorio observes that in calling in the foreign troops, "Kalakaua had won his victory, but it cost him dearly. His mana [divine power] would forever be based on American power and support." In other words, Kalakaua's first act as king-elect was to embody the deepest fears of Queen Emma's numerous supporters. He would have to endure significant native opposition more or less until Emma's death in 1885.

In the first year of his reign Kalakaua traveled to Washington to lobby for a reciprocity treaty allowing Hawaiian sugar to enter the United States tax-free. Kalakaua was the first monarch who ever came to the nation's capital. In honor of the king's visit, President Ulysses S. Grant hosted the very first state dinner.

The king was successful in promoting the treaty and securing Grant's backing, though it took a couple of years for the U.S. Congress to pass the law authorizing it. If the king saw promoting Hawaiian prosperity as the way to uphold the islands' independence, the United States Minister to Hawaii had the opposite view. He told the Senate Committee on Foreign Relations, "If reciprocity of commerce is established between the two countries, there cannot be a doubt that the effect will be to hold those islands with hooks of steel in the interests of the United States, and to result finally in their annexation to the United States."

Hawaiians had worried that a condition for reciprocity would be handing over Pearl Harbor to the United States. An editorial in the Honolulu paper *Nuhou* considered "the Pearl Harbor Cession as an unnecessary measure to secure Reciprocity. . . . It is the interest of America to Americanize us, and she needs no bribe to do so." While Kalakaua retained control of Pearl (for now), he did agree to the American amendment that the treaty prohibited the king from leasing "any port, harbor, or any other territory in his dominions . . . to any other power, state, or government." Jonathan Osorio notes, "That amendment . . . in some ways was more destructive to Hawaiian independence than the actual cession of Hawaiian territory." He continues, "A foreign power assumed the authority to restrict the use and development of the Kingdom's territory, thus compromising the king's sovereignty over it."

Before the reciprocity treaty went into effect, Hawaii exported twenty-six million pounds of sugar a year. Within ten years of the treaty's passage, that number had increased tenfold.

Reciprocity also had a dramatic effect on Hawaii's racial makeup because of the hordes of sugar laborers recruited from China, Japan, Portugal, Korea, and, eventually, the Philippines. According to Ralph Kuykendall, in 1876 Hawaiians and part-Hawaiians comprised nearly 90 percent of the population while Asians were 4.5 percent. In 1900, Asians were nearly 57 percent of the population while Hawaiians, at 26 percent, had become a minority.

Gaylord Kubota's paternal grandfather emigrated from Japan in 1900 at the age of sixteen to work for the Honolulu Sugar Company. Kubota is the retired director of the Alexander & Baldwin Sugar Museum on Maui. He said that soon after he was hired to be the museum's director, in 1983, one of his tasks was to tour the refinery where his grandfather had worked.

Standing in the museum he helped design, he said, "So that's in three generations, from my grandfather to myself. There is this Japanese saying that's really important. It's called *okage sama de.* It means, 'I am who I am because of you.' What it reflects is the debt that you owe to previous generations laying the groundwork for what you accomplished."

Directing my attention to the museum's displays on plantation life, Kubota says, "When you're developing raw land, you have to have workers to develop it. If you're going to bring in workers, you need to provide housing for them. Along with that you need to provide medical care and small stores. So that's how these little plantation towns grew up. And in those days, without automobiles, they were kind of isolated. Sure, distances weren't long by today's standards, but they were if you had to walk. So you have little self-contained communities growing up all over the islands."

Planters deliberately recruited an ethnically diverse workforce, hoping the language barriers would prevent laborers from organizing. One plantation manager advised, "Keep a variety of laborers, that is different nationalities, and thus prevent any concerted action in case of strikes, for there are few, if any, cases of Japs, Chinese, and Portuguese entering into a strike as a unit."

Kubota acknowledges, "They were deliberately segregated." But he hastens to add that most laborers preferred it that way. "It's natural that you're more comfortable with people from your own culture, speaking your own language, having your own customs, and sharing your own foods. That's part of Hawaii's heritage. These cultures were maintained in these camps, but they eventually started cross-fertilizing one another, to the point where they blended. One of the great equalizers was the schools. The public schools had a tremendous role because the kids of the original immigrants would mix with each other quite a bit. And they started to learn to share one another's foods, and things like that." He tells me about a series of oral-history interviews he conducted. In one of them, a woman he describes as "a third- or fourth-generation Portuguese-American was talking about how her family had a standing order from the Japanese neighbor lady for tofu."

I told him about my fondness for plate lunch. "This is called a kau kau tin," he says, pointing to a multilayered metal lunch can. "This is the origin of the mixed plate. The staple would be put in the bottom, like rice, and your entrée would be put in the top. A tradition developed among some [workers] when they got together. They would put the top part in the center of the circle and they would partake of one another's food."

Just as the sugar plantations changed the islands' ethnic makeup, they also profoundly altered the physical landscape. We were talking about Maui's central plain before the advent of commercial agriculture. Kubota says, "Isabella Bird, a traveler in the 1870s, described central Maui as a veritable Sahara in miniature. There were these clouds of sand and dust. That's what central Maui looked like before. And to illustrate that I've taken that picture that shows you the difference between irrigation and no irrigation."

In the photo on display he's referring to, there is a visible line where the irrigated land stops. There the greenery ends and the desert, complete with cactus, begins.

"The plantations started in areas where there was a lot of rainfall," Kubota says of the sugar industry's formative years. In her history of Hawaiian irrigation ditches, *Sugar Water,* Carol Wilcox explains, "Sugar is a thirsty crop. To produce 1 pound of sugar takes 4,000 pounds of water, 500 gallons. One ton of sugar takes 4,000 tons of water, a million gallons. One million gallons of water a day is needed to irrigate 100 acres of sugarcane."

Central Maui, a flat plain between Mount Haleakala and the West Maui Mountains, gets plenty of sunlight but little moisture. The mountains receive plenty of rainfall and groundwater discharge but are inconveniently mountainous.

"You can't really move sunlight, but you can move water," Kubota says.

A Kauai plantation had built an aqueduct to irrigate its fields back in the 1850s. But the irrigation ditches built on Maui soon after the signing of the reciprocity treaty with the United States were as revolutionary to the ecosystem as the overthrow of the monarchy was to the political system. The ditches were probably more revolutionary; replacing a monarchy with an oligarchy is nowhere near as radical as turning a desert green.

As engineering projects, the sugar ditches are impressive. I've hiked along the Waihee Ditch in the West Maui Mountains, following the manmade river uphill. The enormity of the undertaking is apparent in every tunnel, rope bridge, and crook in the trail. It obviously works beautifully — sometimes the water pours down the ditch so fast it churns white. It's a very Book of Genesis hike — passing bamboo groves only to stare at some big pipe vomiting rainwater out of a tricky-looking tunnel; it's obvious that man has subdued this bit of dominion.

These days, because of cheap sugar grown in Asia, the Hawaiian sugar industry is going the way of the mamo bird. On my first trip to Kauai, I went to Waimea to see the beach where Captain Cook first met the Hawaiians in 1778. From the pier, I could see the steam rising from the Gay & Robinson sugar mill nearby. However, in 2009, G&R ended its sugar operations after 120 years. On October 31 of that year, the final cane-haul trucks drove through Waimea past the statue of Captain Cook to unload cane at the mill for the last time. G&R leased some of its cane fields to Dow AgroSciences to grow seed corn. There is talk of ethanol.

That leaves the Maui operations of Hawaii & Commercial Sugar Company, across the street from the sugar museum, as the last operational sugar mill in the Hawaiian Islands. H&CS is a subsidiary of Alexander & Baldwin, a company founded in 1870.

Samuel Thomas Alexander and Henry Perrine Baldwin were both sons of missionaries and Punahou School alums. Alexander married Amos Star Cooke's daughter, and Baldwin married Alexander's sister.

Sam Alexander's father, William, was the

missionary portrayed by the artist from the United States Exploring Expedition preaching in that kukui grove on Kauai. Sam learned about irrigation working in the gardens of the Lahainaluna School after his father was transferred there to teach.

In 1876, after the reciprocity treaty was signed, the Kalakaua government granted Alexander & Baldwin the license to build an irrigation ditch to transport water from Haleakala to their plantation. Baldwin had had his right arm amputated earlier that year when his hand got caught in mill machinery. When his employees balked at descending into a steep gorge to lay a pipe, only after he lowered himself down the rope with his solitary arm did the workers follow suit.

When Gaylord Kubota and I were standing next to the display on Baldwin's entrepreneurial derring-do, he said, "There was actual physical risk in this. The early entrepreneurs didn't have it all easy, they didn't automatically make a lot of money. For Alexander & Baldwin, if they hadn't gotten the water across the ditch they would've lost everything. It would be Spreckels's plantation."

Kubota is referring to Claus Spreckels, the "sugar king of Hawaii." Spreckels, a

German immigrant who supposedly arrived in the United States with a single coin in his pocket, eventually parlayed success as a San Francisco brewer into buying up property in California to raise sugar beets and sugarcane. At the time the reciprocity treaty with Hawaii was signed (to his dismay), he dominated sugar refining in California. Once the treaty went into effect, the opportunistic Spreckels made haste to Hawaii to get in on the coming windfall. His main strategy in insinuating himself into the Hawaiian scene was to cozy up to King Kalakaua.

Spreckels purchased land in Central Maui and requested water rights from the government to build his own ditch. When the cabinet pledged to consider his request at some point, the impatient Spreckels made plans to speed up approval. Which is to say he made plans to play cards with the king. In the wee hours of the Spreckels-Kalakaua game night, royal messengers appeared at cabinet ministers' doors, requesting their resignations. The king appointed a new cabinet and Spreckels received his water rights within the week. Spreckels's biographer, Jacob Adler, remarks that Kalakaua's cashbook contains an entry for $40,000 in promissory notes to the king from Spreckels. "The date of these notes is the same as that of Spreckels's lease of the Maui water rights." He goes on to quote one of the justices of the Hawaii Supreme Court who called the backroom deal "the first time money has been used in this country to procure official favors."

Spreckels's water rights, secured in July of 1878, entitled him to all prior rights to waters unused by that September. In other words, besides the right to build his own ditch, Spreckels could take over Alexander & Baldwin's ditch if it wasn't finished and in use by the September deadline. (A&B met the deadline.)

That initial installment of $40K was only a down payment on the king's soul. Spreckels, Adler notes, would accumulate various nicknames due to his snowballing influence over Kalakaua — from "the uncrowned king of Hawaii" and "the power behind the throne" to "His Royal Saccharinity" and "Herr Von Boss."

Kalakaua's weaknesses and strengths were of a piece. The king had a decidedly antipuritanical strain that might have been a reaction against his childhood deprivation at the Chiefs' Children's School. Recall his sister Liliuokalani's description of the hungry students sneaking out at night just to dig up roots to eat. Is it surprising that one of those students would grow up to host lavish banquets and parties? His aversion to the drab missionary aesthetic was double-edged. On the one hand, Kalakaua drank so much that writer Robert Louis Stevenson once witnessed the king putting away three bottles of champagne and two of brandy in a single afternoon. On the other hand, the king's sensual bent resulted in a true devotion to what he lovingly called the "enchanted by-ways" of Hawaiian customs and folkways the missionaries disdained.

Kalakaua had the ancient creation chant, the *Kumulipo,* transcribed and published; Noenoe Silva argues that the chant "can be read as a political text" in that its account of the history of Hawaii from the beginning of the universe to the genealogies of the high chiefs serves "to legitimize the existence of the nation itself." I am beginning to realize that might be why Kekuni Blaisdell answered my question about the overthrow of the queen in 1893 by going back to the world's creation. He was telling me the story told in the *Kumulipo,* beginning with the births of the taro plant and his brother the first Hawaiian, a story that extends down the generations to Liliuokalani and her brother Kalakaua's ancestors. Maybe Blaisdell was trying to make me understand that to remove the queen from her people in 1893 was to sever a cord so long it stretched back to the beginning of time.

As a champion of the old traditions, Kalakaua inspired a reawakening of Hawaiian nationalism. His most important cultural legacy might be his revival of the hula, the native art form despised by missionaries and outlawed by Queen Kaahumanu when she converted to Christianity. In the half century that followed, hula had gone underground. In 1883, nine years into his reign, Kalakaua organized coronation festivities for himself and his wife on the grounds of the newly built Iolani Palace. Along with luaus and the unveiling of a new statue of Kamehameha the Great, which still stands across the street from the palace, hula performances were featured prominently in the two weeks of royal shindigs.

Kalakaua is still beloved by hula dancers, who perform and compete every year on the Big Island at the Merrie Monarch Festival named in his honor. My hula dancer friend from Maui, John-Mario Sevilla, told me that there is also "a flaired, almost flamboyant hula step named after him." John-Mario contends, "When he placed the hula at the center of his corona-tion, Kalakaua made a significant gesture to the past, which is where Hawaiians tradi-tionally looked for truth and meaning, in the face of rapid contemporary change. By challenging the foreign shame of the hula, he popularized and, therefore, politicized it. It's as if he decided to write and publish books after all the libraries had been burned. Like surfing, he recognized that hula was organically, soulfully, metaphysi-cally, irrepressibly Hawaiian. Because of him, today we have some of the earliest documentation of much of the *hula kahiko,* the ancient canon."

A missionary descendant, William R. Castle, held on to his forebears' disdain for the art form and insisted that the printers who published the coronation program of the hula chants be arrested for obscenity. One of the issues was the inclusion of hula maʻi, the traditional songs praising a chief's genitals. Noenoe Silva points out that the sexuality of these hula was meaningful to the king and his people because the natives "had suffered depopulation caused by epidemics of foreign disease and also by childlessness."

If anything, the hula maʻi performed at the coronation must have been the opposite of obscene: those songs must have seemed all the more poignant to the natives, given that Kalakaua and his wife, Kapiolani, were childless, that Kalakaua's very election as king depended on the demise of the Kamehameha line, and that yet another smallpox outbreak, two years earlier, in 1881, had killed more than seven hundred people.

In her memoir, Kalakaua's sister, Liliuokalani, recalls of the coronation: "It was wise and patriotic to spend money to awaken in the people a national pride."

The money was a sticking point with the haole-businessmen subset of the kingdom's taxpayers, who were growing increasingly irate about the king's expenditures. You don't earn the nickname "Merrie Monarch" by sticking to a budget. The attorney Sanford Dole attended the coronation with his wife, Anna, who wrote her sister, "It was a glorious day with much pageantry. Sanford did not enjoy it as much as I did because he worried about the money."

An editorial in *Planters' Monthly,* the sugar planters' trade periodical, complained, "The so-called Coronation of the King, with the attendant follies and extravagances, has been directly damaging to the property interests and welfare of the country. It has been demoralizing in its influence, and productive only of harm."

Lawyer Lorrin Thurston noted in his *Memoirs of the Hawaiian Revolution,* "The appropriation for the coronation of Kalakaua and Kapiolani was $10,000; but the report of the committee showed that the expenditures exceeded $33,000." Thurston also felt that the hula performances spoke to the king's "inherent filth of mind and utter lack of decency and moral sense."

In 1884, Kalakaua, perhaps chastened by complaints of government extravagance, sent a message to the legislature, advising lawmakers to cut spending appropriations "commencing from the head of the Civil List or Privy Purse," which is to say the king's personal allowance. His subjects were so pleased they threw the king a parade and, Kuykendall writes, "For a time, economy was the watchword," though in the end, he adds, the king ended up approving a budget about $1.5 million in the red.

Missionary descendants Sanford Dole and W. R. Castle were elected to the legislature in 1884, and Lorrin Thurston joined them in 1886. All three were attorneys and graduates of the Punahou School; Dole, whose father was its founding teacher, was born on the school's grounds. Castle's missionary father had founded the firm of Castle and Cooke together with Amos Starr Cooke of the Chiefs' Children's School. Thurston was missionary stock twice over, being the grandson of Asa and Lucy Thurston from the pioneer company on his father's side as well as having as his maternal grandfather Lorrin Andrews, the founding teacher of the Lahainaluna School. All three were sent to schools in the United States — Dole to the Protestant stronghold Williams College; Castle to Oberlin College, then Harvard Law; and Thurston to Columbia University's law school, where Theodore Roosevelt was his classmate.

Dole, Castle, and Thurston were ringleaders in the haole political movement known variously as the Reform Party, the Independents (as in independent from the king), and, somewhat pejoratively, the Missionary Party. They were allied with the white planters scattered around the islands, but the growing opposition to the king was clearly focused within the Honolulu business community that provided supplies, legal services, and financing to the planters, spearheaded by the attorneys, and by Thurston in particular.

In 1884, the year after Kalakaua's coronation, another missionary descendant, Sereno E. Bishop, wrote an article in *Hawaiian*

Monthly describing Hawaii as "a state where foreigners conducted all the business of the country, and the native race still continued to exercise the sovereignty." Bishop concluded, "The base of the throne is decayed, and no severe shock will be awaited to topple it over."

The electorate, along with the legislature, was overwhelmingly Hawaiian, while haoles paid a majority of the kingdom's taxes. Which makes sense considering they controlled a majority of the kingdom's lands and were making the majority of the kingdom's profits. But if history teaches us anything, upper-class white guys can be exceedingly touchy about taxation. Lorrin Thurston recalled of the election of 1886, "Of the twenty-eight elected members of the House of Representatives, only nine were independent of royal control." That number included himself, along with Castle and Dole.

Looking back on the rise to power of this circle of missionary descendants in *Hawaii's Story by Hawaii's Queen,* Liliuokalani concludes,

Although settled among us, and drawing their wealth from our resources, they were alien to us in their customs and ideas respecting government, and desired above all things the extension of their power, and to carry out their own special plans of advancement, and to secure their own personal benefit. It may be true that they really believed us unfit to be trusted to administer the growing wealth of the Islands in a safe and proper way. But if we manifested any incompetency, it was in not foreseeing that they would be bound by no obligations, by honor, or by oath of allegiance, should an opportunity arise for seizing our country, and bringing it under the authority of the United States.

Alas, a failure to predict the missionary boys' capacity for treason was not the sole incompetency of Liliuokalani's brother's administration. The fact is, Kalakaua could be corrupt and inept.

The historian (and son of missionaries) William De Witt Alexander asserts, "The election of 1886 was the most corrupt one ever held in this Kingdom. . . . During the canvass the country districts were flooded with cheap gin, chiefly furnished by the King, who paid for it by franking other liquor through the Custom House free of duty." This royal liquor, nicknamed "election gin," was ladled out in exchange for votes for legislative candidates loyal to the king.

Though after the reciprocity treaty went into effect the kingdom had never been richer, the king's spending habits and gambling losses put the government in debt continually, with half the deficit owed to Claus Spreckels. For his trouble, the sugar king received special treatment including kickbacks like a healthy (yet unnecessary) commission brokering the minting of Kalakaua coins in the United States, an ill-conceived vanity currency bearing the king's head in profile.

Kalakaua's crony-in-chief and the executor and instigator of many of his most questionable decisions was the man he eventually appointed as his premier, the haole yes-man Walter Murray Gibson. Often described as an "adventurer," Gibson arrived in Hawaii from Utah in 1861. A recent convert to Mormonism (or so he pretended), Gibson had been sent to the Pacific with the blessings of Brigham Young. Not that mere Mormonism could contain the multitudes of Gibson's ambitions.

Gibson was born in 1822, the child of English sheepherders. As a boy, he immigrated with his family to Canada, then to

New York. The teenage Gibson made his way to South Carolina, where he married young. By the time he was twenty-one, he was a widower and father of three. "I wanted to fly on the wings of the wind toward the rising sun," he later wrote. Which is a poetic way of saying he ditched his kids with his dead wife's relatives and lit out on a life of adventure inspired by, he claimed, an uncle who had sailed to Malaysia while working for an Arab merchant. Gibson recalled, "He talked of Arabia, and of the islands of the far East: and more than all of Sumatra: of the perfumes that wafted from her shores; of the many dainty fruits, and myriad bright-feathered birds of her flowery groves."

Gibson's dream was to move to a Pacific island, found his own kingdom, then start expanding his domain into an empire. To that end, he traveled to his uncle's old stomping grounds, the Dutch colony of Sumatra. Upon arrival, Gibson wrote a letter to a local sultan, offering help if the sultan felt like rising up against his Dutch overlords. Said letter was intercepted by Dutch officials who imprisoned Gibson for treason on the island of Java. Gibson escaped and made his way back to the United States, where he wrote a flowery memoir of his incarceration, *The Prisoner of Weltevreden.*

Gibson bounced around, earning a living on the lecture circuit and hounding congressmen and diplomats to help in his ultimately unsuccessful lawsuit against the government of the Netherlands. Passing through Liverpool, Gibson made such an impression on the American consul, Nathaniel Hawthorne, that Hawthorne wrote about him in his book *Our Old Home,* "There was an Oriental fragrance breathing through his talk and an odor of the Spice Islands still lingering in his garments." Still, Hawthorne wasn't sure whether Gibson's tall tales were to be believed. Gibson claimed to have been born at sea to a noblewoman but switched at birth with a peasant baby born the same night, and so he felt robbed of the finery of his birthright. "One looks into his eyes, to see whether he is sane or no," Hawthorne recalled.

In Washington, when Gibson was stalking congressmen to support his claim against the Dutch, he met the Mormon delegate from Utah Territory and cooked up a scheme to resettle the Mormons, then in the throes of troubles with the American government, in the Pacific, perhaps in New Guinea, not that Gibson knew the first thing about New Guinea. Gibson wrote a letter to Brigham Young, claiming, "While I lay in a dungeon in the island of Java, a voice said to me: 'You shall show the way to a people, who shall build up a kingdom in these isles, whose lines of power shall run around the earth.' "

Gibson, now reunited with his daughter Talula, traveled to Salt Lake City in 1860 and converted to Mormonism there. He convinced Young to send him to the Pacific, starting with Japan and perhaps going on to the Philippines and Malaysia, to investigate the potential for Mormon missions and/or settlements. En route, the Gibsons stopped in Hawaii and, like a lot of people who pass through Hawaii, they fell in love with the place and stuck around.

Mormon missionaries had been sent to Hawaii in 1850 but were recalled to Salt Lake in 1857 during the so-called Utah War, a standoff between Mormons and the U.S. Army when President Buchanan replaced Brigham Young as governor of Utah Territory with a non-Mormon.

There were a few hundred native converts to Mormonism in the islands when Gibson arrived in 1861. Many of them had settled on the small island of Lanai in a weedy volcanic crater called the Palawai Basin.

When Gibson saw Palawai for the first time, he wrote in his diary, "I said to myself I will plant my stakes here and make a home for the rest of my days." He planned to "fill this lovely crater with corn and wine and oil and babies and love and health and brotherly rejoicing and sisterly kisses and the memory of me for evermore." (Eventually, Gibson's historical status did warrant a plaque on the side of the road in Palawai, but, as Kepa Maly of the Lanai Culture & Heritage Center told me, "People on Lanai today almost have no memory, no recollection of him at all.")

Looking upon Palawai now, a golden grassy stretch of empty land crossed by a forlorn single file of pines along a road, the depth of Gibson's vision, or perhaps delusion, becomes clear. He dreamed that "Lines of power shall radiate from this shining crater. I set up my standard here and it goes hence to the islands of the sea. Lanai shall be famous in Malaysia, in Oceania." To think Lanai could become the seat of a Pacific empire when it's never even been a county seat.

Kepa Maly told me, "Lanai has always, politically, environmentally, religiously, socially, sat in the shadow of Maui." That is true, except for Lanai's place in Walter Murray Gibson's head.

With his connection to Brigham Young, Gibson quickly took charge of the Hawaiian Mormons, joining the ones eking out a living on Lanai and attracting the others scattered around the islands. He dressed in long white robes and called himself the High Priest of Melchizedek and tried to turn Lanai into his own private Waco. He stored his copy of the Book of Mormon inside a hollow rock and told his flock God would strike them dead if they dared to touch it. "The people are poor; in pocket, in brain, in everything," he confided in his diary. Still, he said, "It is a little kingdom of love and worship."

Gibson solicited donations from his flock, purchasing and leasing more and more land on Lanai, always putting the titles in his name. He also funded his real estate holdings by selling church offices to parishioners, a heresy. Salt Lake got wind of his deviations from Mormon orthodoxy. Headquarters dispatched a fact-finding team in 1864 to investigate rumors of impropriety. Once they learned of Gibson's side business selling church titles to believers and rescued the Book of Mormon from the hollow rock (without being struck dead), they excommunicated Gibson and asked him to turn over the land titles to the church; he refused. The church then abandoned Lanai and moved to the town of Laie, in northeastern Oahu, where it continues to thrive — Brigham Young University-Hawaii has a campus there.

Gibson stayed on Lanai for a few years, his only subjects being a flock of sheep. He became a Hawaiian citizen in 1866. In 1873, he started a bilingual newspaper published in Honolulu, *Nuhou*. His biographer, Jacob Adler, wrote, "Gibson cast the descendants of the missionary families and their business associates as Americanizers, basically unaccepting of a Hawaiian culture or a government under a Hawaiian king who was more than a figurehead." Gibson had become fluent in Hawaiian back in his days as a quasi-Mormon prophet. Adler continues, "Upon himself he put the mantle of champion, the defender of the native kingdom from the Americanizers." It says something about Gibson's powers of persuasion that an American could successfully cast himself as the natives' champion opposing Americanization.

Of course, that tactic did not endear Gibson to the haole community. Gibson threw in his lot with David Kalakaua, using his newspaper to promote Kalakaua's election as king.

Approving of Kalakaua's pledge to "Increase the Nation," a *Nuhou* editorial proclaimed: "Let maternity in every class be honored; — and the cries of babies be more esteemed than even the tuneful chants of churches. . . . Let King Kalakaua have children, come how they may, to fill up his Kingdom."

In 1878, Gibson ran for a seat in the legislature and won. He led the charge to build a new palace in Honolulu.

In 1882, Kalakaua appointed Gibson Hawaii's premier, the office second in importance only to that of king. Finally, at the age of sixty, Gibson's dream of running a Pacific kingdom had come true — or close enough. And, just as he had always seen a kingdom as a stepping-stone to empire, Gibson convinced Kalakaua to think bigger than Hawaii, to ponder Hawaii as the seat of a Polynesian empire. Gibson referred to the plan as "Primacy in the Pacific." The government dispatched envoy John E. Bush to Samoa to suss out a Samoan chief's interest in a confederation. Nothing concrete ever came of the plan but Bush's letters back to Honolulu that are stored in the Hawaii State Archives are interesting in that a Hawaiian government official (of Hawaiian descent) questions the Samoans' capacity for self-government, speaking in the same patronizing tone in which American imperialists dismissed the capacity for self-government of all the island acquisitions of 1898, Hawaii included. Bush wrote Gibson, "The past history of Samoa has shown that the people cannot govern themselves in modern methods without outside help. . . . A strong native government with intelligent foreign supervision that would make good laws and have the power to enforce them would be best for Samoa."

The Primacy plan accomplished nothing but riling up Germany, a country in the process of colonizing part of Samoa. The crown's judgment was once again called into question.

King Kalakaua's most damaging scandal was probably his behavior regarding the government license to import opium. The drug had been introduced to Hawaii by Chinese laborers. The Englishwoman Isabella Bird witnessed sugar plantation workers in Hilo smoking it in 1873. Plantation work was hard and monotonous. In his book on plantation life, *Pau Hana,* Ronald Takaki writes, "A Chinese plantation worker recalled how the cook for his gang would bring their hot lunches to the field: 'In the top of the bucket [lunch pail] was a little paper or envelope with the dope in it. All the men . . . took their dope that way with their dinner.' "

Opium became illegal in Hawaii in 1874. Lorrin Thurston recalled of his freshman term in the House of Representatives: "In the 1886 session of the Legislature, a member of the Royal Ticket introduced a bill, at the direct instigation of Kalakaua to license the sale of opium and to sell a license for a fixed sum." The bill was opposed by the haoles of the Independent or Reform Party, including Sanford Dole, who later described it as "inconsistent with the public welfare." Still, it passed.

Kalakaua sold the license to import opium to a Chinese merchant for $71,000. The king collected the fee, then failed to give the merchant the license. Then the king charged a second Chinese merchant the same fee; the second merchant wouldn't pay up until he got the license. When the first merchant asked the king to repay him the fee for a license he never received, the king refused and pocketed the money.

All of Gibson and Kalakaua's mishaps and misjudgments were adding up. In January of 1887 some haole businessmen, led by Lorrin Thurston, formed a secret organization called the Hawaiian League, which Thurston later described as "an outgrowth of a revolt in the public mind of Hawaii against the aggressions, extravagance, and debaucheries of the Kalakaua regime." Thurston described its genesis:

On the day after Christmas, 1886, as I stood at the front gate of my residence on Judd Street, near Nuuanu, Dr. S.G. Tucker, a homeopathic physician, drew up in his buggy and said: "Thurston, how long are we going to stand this kind of thing?" "What kind of thing?" I inquired. He replied: "The running away with the community by Kalakaua, his interference with elections, and running the Legislature for his own benefit, and all that." "Well," said I, "what can we do about it?" "I suggest," Dr. Tucker answered, "that we form an organization, including all nationalities, which shall force him to be decent, and reign, not rule, or take the consequences." After some discussion, I said I would consider the idea.

By "all nationalities" Tucker meant Anglo *and* Saxon — Americans, Brits, perhaps the odd German or Canadian. Thurston goes on to say that that afternoon he went to the house of his law partner and fellow Punahou alum William A. Kinney and discussed Tucker's suggestion. Kinney, whom Thurston describes as "more belligerent than Dr. Tucker or I," showed Thurston a book from his library about the French Revolution. "He got the book and pointed out the declaration made by the revolutionists and some of their orders. Among others, one called upon citizens in sympathy with the revolutionists to declare themselves, and requested that all arms be turned in to support the revolution."

Thurston then started secretly fomenting revolt, recruiting, among others, Sanford Dole, William R. Castle, and Nathaniel Bright Emerson. Emerson, a physician, was, like Thurston, Castle, and Dole, the son of missionaries and a Punahou grad. His evangelist parents founded the Oahu town of Haleiwa on the North Shore, now a hippie surfer hangout; the church they built was renamed after Queen Liliuokalani and still stands across Kamehameha Highway from the famous frozen-dessert stand Matsumoto Shave Ice. Emerson was born in Hawaii and attended Dole's alma mater, Williams College. He served in a Massachusetts regiment of the Union Army at

Gettysburg and Chancellorsville, where he was wounded. He would go on to translate David Malo's *Hawaiian Antiquities* and author a relatively appreciative book about hula called *The Unwritten Literature of Hawaii.* (Though Noenoe Silva noticed that in Emerson's copy of the program of hula chants for Kalakaua's coronation — the one that got its printers charged with obscenity — Emerson's marginal notes next to a genital-celebration song includes the assessment "smut.")

The missionary descendants in the Hawaiian League were just as historically minded as Kalakaua. The king was reasserting the Hawaiian past through his patronage of hula and his publication of the *Kumulipo,* the creation chant linking his own chiefly ancestors all the way back to the planet's dark beginning, to "the slime which established the earth." But as a letter published in the May 31, 1887, edition of the haole mouthpiece the *Hawaiian Gazette* would put it, "Some of the descendants of the men who forced King John to give the English people the Magna Charta are here. The descendants of those who fought on Bunker Hill are with us." The Magna Carta, the Revolutionary War — these are akin to the *Kumulipo* in that they are the creation stories of Anglo-American freedom, expressions of the belief that the king is not above the law of the land, the belief that subjects dissatisfied with their king should rebuke him, sever their ties to his throne.

The mission statement of the Hawaiian League, as remembered by Lorrin Thurston, borrows from the Declaration of Independence: "The Hawaiian League is a voluntary organization, organized to secure efficient, decent and honest government in Hawaii. To the securing and maintenance of government of this character, we do hereby pledge our lives, our property, and our sacred honor." (Though Thomas Jefferson, John Adams, Ben Franklin, and their coconspirators who signed the Declaration pledged "our lives, our fortunes and our sacred honor," not their property, property being the precise obsession of the Honolulu rebels.)

Sanford Dole: "When the plans became more definite and the support more assured, the league management took measures to arm its members." They purchased guns from local hardware stores as well as ordering a shipment of Springfield rifles.

In June of 1887, the news broke of Kalakaua's opium license swindle, and this emboldened the League to embarrass the king into dismissing his cabinet, including Walter Murray Gibson. In his diary Gibson writes, "Rumors of armed mob, purpose to lynch me." Gibson was forced to flee to San Francisco, where he would die soon thereafter.

Meanwhile, the Hawaiian League held a rally in Honolulu on June 30. The *Hawaiian Gazette* called it a "great reform meeting" in which "one designing mind" called the Hawaiian constitution a "worthless rag."

The *Gazette* reported Thurston's address to the gathering:

> Gentlemen, you and I have been waiting a long time for this day, but it has come. . . . I am here to speak as a Hawaiian. My ancestors came here in the reign of Kamehameha I. I was born and brought up here, and I mean to die here. Hawaii is good enough for me. We all remember the King's message to the legislature in 1884, recommending economy, and asking that it should begin with His Majesty's privy purse . . . but it was followed by appropriations enormously in excess of the revenue. . . . It is not sufficient to have the King accept these resolutions; we must have a new Constitution, and must have it now.

Thurston pointed out that if the king and the people agreed to change the Constitution, then that would not constitute a revolution. But another member of the League, Cecil Brown, put forth the ominous claim that "if Queen Victoria were to act as badly as Kalakaua, she would not live an hour."

Thurston got cracking, writing a new constitution severely limiting the powers of the crown and narrowing voter eligibility. The king was no longer allowed to appoint his own cabinet, and his decisions had to be approved by the cabinet forced upon him. The king was also no longer allowed to appoint members of the House of Nobles. Candidates and voters for the House of Nobles had to own property worth $3,000 or receive yearly incomes of $600; about two-thirds of native Hawaiians of voting age neither owned nor earned that much and so were disqualified from electing representatives in the upper house of their own legislature. If the king vetoed a bill passed by the legislature, the lawmakers could overrule him with a two-thirds majority. Voters were required to be of Hawaiian or European descent and literate in Hawaiian or a European language, including English.

In other words, the new charter barred

the Chinese and Japanese from voting, which was significant, given that they were rapidly becoming the islands' most numerous ethnic groups. This development, Jonathan Osorio points out, marked "the very first time that democratic rights were determined by race in any Hawaiian constitution."

On July 6, the League bullied King Kalakaua into signing the paper reducing his office to that of figurehead. The document was nicknamed the "Bayonet Constitution." If the king had refused to cooperate with his usurpers, Sanford Dole had written to his brother beforehand, "He will be promptly attacked, and a republic probably declared." The cabinet Kalakaua was forced to accept included Lorrin Thurston as minister of the interior.

Liliuokalani, who was away from home, attending Queen Victoria's Jubilee celebration in Great Britain, would later describe her brother's depantsing as "the overthrow of the monarchy." She was right: Hawaiian control of Hawaii was effectively over for good.

Picturing the moment King Kalakaua was coerced into signing Lorrin Thurston's new constitution, I cannot help but remember the first interaction between Thurston's grandmother, Lucy, and Hawaiians sixty-seven years earlier: natives paddling their canoes alongside the *Thaddeus,* passing her a banana through the porthole. She handed them biscuits in return, and they called her "wahine makai," good woman. She wrote, "That interview through the cabin window of the brig *Thaddeus* gave me a strengthening touch in crossing the threshold of the nation."

That cordial, welcoming exchange in 1820 led to this one in 1887, which is all the more frustrating to contemplate because Lucy Thurston's arrogant, disenfranchising grandson and his coconspirators sort of kind of had a point. If Kalakaua had taken better care of his charge, been more mindful of just how fragile his tiny nation's independence was, if he had led with restraint and probity, if he had spent less, drunk less, gambled less, steered clear of that petty, greedy opium con, then his enemies would have been unable to swaddle themselves and their undemocratic motives in the mantle of the Magna Carta and 1776.

Thurston, the Bayonet Constitution's mastermind (and beneficiary), wrote, "Unquestionably the constitution was not in accordance with law; neither was the Declaration of Independence from Great Britain.

Both were revolutionary documents, which had to be forcibly effected and forcibly maintained."

In the fall of 1887, the Thurston cabinet signed off on the renewal of the reciprocity treaty with the United States, with one significant amendment — Pearl Harbor was ceded to the U.S. to use as a naval coaling station. In other words, within one year, working-class Hawaiians had been denied the right to vote for half the legislature, the Hawaiian king became the puppet of a white oligarchy, and one of the archipelago's best ports was handed over to a foreign government.

In 1889, an ailing Kalakaua left for California, hoping to revive his health. He died at the Palace Hotel in San Francisco. His old friend Claus Spreckels attended his deathbed.

At Iolani Palace, Kalakaua's coffin lay in state in the throne room, draped in Princess Nahi'ena'ena's feather skirt, the skirt that had been woven to symbolize the hoped-for fertility of the Kamehameha line.

Liliuokalani was sworn in as queen on January 29, 1891. She was fifty-two. Childless, she named her niece, Princess Kaiulani, as her heir.

When Liliuokalani was sworn in, the McKinley Tariff Act of 1890 threatened Hawaii's livelihood. The reciprocity treaty was still technically in effect. But the McKinley bill, named for its sponsor, Ohio congressman William McKinley, negated Hawaiian sugar's favored status by canceling all foreign sugar tariffs and subsidizing American sugar at two cents per pound. This development erased Hawaii's leg up over sugar produced outside the U.S. and made it more difficult to compete with America's domestic sugar.

To the planters, annexation to the United States — thus making Hawaiian sugar American sugar — seemed like the best fix. The usual haole suspects, once again led by Lorrin A. Thurston, formed a secret organization called the Annexation Club. Thurston, who was scheduled to travel to the States to attend meetings in Chicago about a Hawaiian exhibit at the 1893 World's Columbian Exposition, made a side trip to Washington, D.C., to investigate the American government's willingness to acquire Hawaii. President Benjamin Harrison sent Thurston a message via Secretary of the Navy Benjamin Franklin Tracy, who promised, "If conditions in Hawaii compel you people to act as you have indicated, and you come to Washington with an annexation proposition, you will find an exceedingly sympathetic administration here."

Meanwhile, Queen Liliuokalani had secret plans of her own. In her memoir, she describes receiving a series of visits by well-respected Hawaiians beseeching her to establish a new constitution. She names Joseph Nawahi as one of her visitors. Nawahi, a Lahainaluna-educated lawyer and newspaper editor who was elected to the legislature in 1872, had been one of the Hawaiians opposing her brother early in his reign, condemning reciprocity as "a nation-snatching treaty" that would cause "the throne to be deprived of powers that it has always held as fundamental." After the signing of the Bayonet Constitution, Nawahi had joined a new native Hawaiian political association, Hui Kalai'aina, devoted to amending the loathed constitution and loosening the property requirements so as to allow unfettered suffrage. And so, when Nawahi and others, the queen recalls, "called my attention to the same public need . . . I began to give the subject my careful consideration." Then, she continues, during the legislative election of 1892, "Petitions poured in from every part of the Islands for a new constitution; these were addressed to myself as the reigning sovereign." She estimated that the petitions were signed by 6,500, or two-thirds, of the registered voters. "To have ignored or disregarded so general a request I must have been deaf to the voice of the people, which tradition tells us is the voice of God. No true Hawaiian chief would have done other than to promise a consideration of their wishes."

She wrote a new constitution that would restore the crown's lost powers and expand her subjects' voting rights, presenting it to her cabinet on January 14, 1893. The cabinet convinced her to wait a couple of weeks so they could discuss it. A crowd had gathered in front of Iolani Palace and she addressed them in Hawaiian from the lanai, promising to present them with a new constitution soon.

Hearing this news, Lorrin Thurston started consulting members of the Annexation Club. A hundred or so of his cohorts composed and signed an open letter, since lost. In *Memoirs of the Hawaiian Revolution,* Thurston remembered the gist of it this way: "Since Liliuokalani had announced her intention of subverting the constitution and arbitrarily promulgating a new one, the undersigned declared her to be in attempted revolution against the constitution and government, and pledged their support to the cabinet in resisting her."

The irony of constitutional revolutionaries complaining about a possible constitutional revolution was lost on Thurston. Moreover, for the queen to present a new constitution to her cabinet was in fact legal according to the Bayonet Constitution — she simply needed the cabinet's approval, which is why the ministers asked her for time to consider her proposals.

Nevertheless, Thurston organized a "committee of safety" and argued that "the solution of the present situation is annexation to the United States." He called on the United States Minister to Hawaii, John L. Stevens, to seek the diplomat's support. Thurston then informed his coconspirators that Stevens had reassured him that the USS *Boston,* a naval cruiser, was in the harbor and at the ready to land troops "to prevent the destruction of American life and property, and in regard to the matter of establishing a Provisional Government they of course would recognize the existing government whatever it might be." Meaning, if the committee took control of the government, Minister Stevens would formally recognize that new government as legitimate.

Dueling mass meetings were held by both royalists and antiroyalists. On January 16, troops from the *Boston* marched into Honolulu to guard the American consulate. That night the Committee of Safety asked Sanford Dole to serve as the president of the forthcoming new government — which they thought of as a temp job until American annexation went through. Dole balked and asked them if they would consider ousting Liliuokalani and installing her heir and niece, Princess Kaiulani, as the new queen. They refused. The next morning, January 17, Dole accepted.

That afternoon the Committee of Safety occupied the government office building across the street from Iolani Palace while the cabinet ministers loyal to the queen were out trying to secure aid from Minister Stevens, unaware that the diplomat had sided with their opponents. Once Stevens received word that the revolutionaries were in place, he issued a statement on behalf of the U.S. government, recognizing the new provisional government "as the *de facto* Government of the Hawaiian Islands."

Upon hearing this news, the queen issued a statement of protest: "That I yield to the superior force of the United States of

America, whose minister plenipotentiary, His Excellency John L. Stevens, has caused United States troops to be landed at Honolulu and declared that he would support the said provisional government."

In other words, Liliuokalani surrendered, but not to her usurpers — only to the American government, and only temporarily. Her statement continues that she will "yield my authority until such time as the Government of the United States shall, upon the facts being presented to it, undo the action of its representatives and reinstate me in the authority which I claim as the constitutional sovereign of the Hawaiian Islands."

That night Dole and his new cabal of administrators met and decided to dispatch a delegation to Washington to lobby for annexation forthwith. Among the travel party: Lorrin Thurston and William R. Castle. They had no trouble convincing President Benjamin Harrison to submit a treaty of annexation to the U.S. Senate. But the treaty was not ratified before the inauguration of Harrison's successor, the Democrat Grover Cleveland, in March of 1893.

Cleveland withdrew the treaty, pending an investigation. He sent Congressman James H. Blount to Hawaii to look into the overthrow. Upon arrival in Honolulu, Blount lowered the American flag the Dole administration had raised.

Native political organizations, including the Hawaiian Patriotic League, submitted petitions to Blount, and a plea to pass along to Cleveland lamenting, "The fate of our little kingdom and its inhabitants is in your hands."

Blount reported back to the president a number of troubling facts, most notably that a majority of native Hawaiians opposed American annexation and were adamant about wanting their queen back in power. Ultimately Blount concluded that the American Minister had colluded with the architects of the coup and sent American troops to back the revolution.

Based on Blount's findings, Cleveland submitted a message to Congress in December 1893, noting,

But for the lawless occupation of Honolulu under false pretexts by the United States forces, and but for Minister Stevens' recognition of the provisional government when the United States forces were its sole support and constituted its only military strength, the Queen and her Government would never have yielded to the provisional government, even for a time and for the sole purpose of submitting her case to the enlightened justice of the United States.

Cleveland proclaimed, "I shall not again submit the treaty of annexation to the Senate for its consideration."

The Cleveland administration sent a request to the Dole government to restore the queen to the throne. The Dole administration replied, "We do not recognize the right of the President of the United States to interfere with our domestic affairs. Such right could be conferred upon him by the act of this government, and by that alone, or it could be acquired by conquest." By which they meant that the only way Liliuokalani was regaining her throne was at gunpoint. Cleveland passed the buck, turning the matter over to the Congress.

Congress held hearings about the Hawaiian situation chaired by Senator John Tyler Morgan, Democrat of Alabama. The Morgan Report, as the committee's findings became known, contradicted the Blount Report. On the subject of the restoration of Queen Liliuokalani, the Morgan Report proclaims, "When a crown falls, in any kingdom of the Western Hemisphere, it is pulverized, and when a scepter departs, it departs forever." It goes on to conclude that the American people would not "sustain any American ruler" in restoring any monarch "no matter how virtuous and sincere the reasons may be that seem to justify him."

Thurston, quoting that passage to one of his cronies, surmised in a letter that "it may be taken as the definite crystallization of the sentiment of Congress on the subject." In other words, the American Congress was never going to send troops to restore the queen. The Dole oligarchy was safe.

Still, the Provisional Government men realized that Cleveland would not budge on annexation. They would have to wait until at least the end of the president's term to hand over Hawaii to the United States. Accepting that fact, they needed to hunker down and establish a more permanent government. When it came time for the oligarchs to frame a constitution for their new country, Lorrin Thurston wrote Sanford Dole a letter on March 10, 1894, with his thoughts on the subject. It reads so much like a long Randy Newman song sung from the point of view of an uppity, powerful white man delighting in his own self-importance that I can't peruse Thurston's words without hearing Newman's piano accompaniment twinkling in my head. Thurston writes, "I hope that those who are drafting the constitution will not allow fine theories of free government to predominate over the necessities of the present situation." He counsels against free speech because that would only encourage the native opposition: "To treat them with forbearance and courtesy is like trying to disinfect leprosy with rose water." He casually dismisses the need to guarantee a trial by jury, which had only been a bedrock legal principle in the English-speaking world for, oh, nearly seven hundred years. (When one of Thurston's fellow revolutionaries in 1887 bragged to the *Hawaiian Gazette* that the descendants of the men behind the Magna Carta had settled in Hawaii, apparently that did not mean they wanted to actually abide by the Great Charter's holiest guarantee.)

Thurston simply points out, "We may get into such a condition that all trials will be a farce." You know, the sort of farce where a jury of an accused's peers finds against the interests of the oligarchy.

Freedom of the press? "I feel that the power to suppress the revolutionary press and to deport conspirators are the key to the present situation," Thurston concludes.

Thurston also touches on the idea of

requiring a loyalty oath to those participating in the constitutional convention. He sees two advantages in this prerequisite. First: "To finally impress upon the world, and more particularly the Kanaka [i.e., native] mind the fact that monarchy is *pau* [finished]." Second: "To so far as possible shut out from participation in the reorganization of the government all those who are not with us."

He was proven wildly correct in his second assumption. The vast majority of the native minority who were allowed to vote refused to pledge an oath of loyalty to a government they despised, thus cutting themselves out of the political process.

And what were they to call this new, ridiculous country? Thurston proposed, "I think that whatever else it is called it should have the word 'Republic' in the name." He wanted Hawaii to be called a republic without it actually being one.

Also: "I do not think that under the existing conditions we are safe in leaving election of President to a popular vote."

Regarding the possibility of female suffrage: nope. After all, "Even in liberty-loving Massachusetts over one half of the population is disenfranched." (Though in a letter to Dole later that month, he changes his

mind about this, adding that women's suffrage "has grown on me." He sees the
advantage of beefing up the puny white
minority with "a large number of the lady
teachers" and "the wives of nearly all the
prominent citizens.")

Finally, voters for senators should be
restricted "absolutely to those who can
speak, read and write the English language."
In this, Thurston suggests that Dole track
down a copy of the new Mississippi state
constitution, because this post-
Reconstruction Jim Crow masterpiece had
figured out innovative ways to deny blacks
the right to vote that the Dole government
could apply to native Hawaiians. Thurston
believes they could go further, refining Mississippi's requirement that a voter should
understand the constitution with a Hawaiian update in which "the voter be able to
write correctly from dictation any portion
of the constitution."

Thurston notes, "This limitation of the
electorate is of course going to raise a great
howl from many of the natives." Whiners.

In response to the founding of the ironi-
cally named Republic of Hawaii, native
Hawaiians did organize a counterrevolution.
This movement succeeded only in getting
Queen Liliuokalani accused of treason. The

Dole government locked her up on the second floor of Iolani Palace and coerced her into signing an agreement to abdicate the throne by threatening to execute the royalists who were captured and jailed. In her memoir, Liliuokalani complains, "For myself, I would have chosen death rather than to have signed it; but it was represented to me that by my signing this paper all the persons who had been arrested, all my people now in trouble by reason of their love and loyalty towards me, would be immediately released."

During the eight months of her incarceration, besides sewing the quilt that is still on display in the room where she was held, she wrote songs as well as an English translation of the *Kumulipo,* the ancient Hawaiian chant that, as she notes, "chronicles the creation of the world and of living creatures, from the shell-fish to the human race." In her introduction to the chant's publication she points out that it was sung to Captain Cook at the temple at Kealakekua Bay. (This is the same temple, by the way, where Henry Obookiah's uncle had been a priest.) She adds that "connecting the earlier kings of ancient history with the monarchs latest upon the throne this chant is a contribution to the history of the Hawaiian Islands." It was also a subtle protest against her jailers. Linking the reign of herself and her brother before her back through time to "the time when the heavens turned and changed," she was taking a stand and, perhaps, mourning the eons of tradition that had been overturned.

In 1890, the year before Liliuokalani assumed the throne, Captain Alfred Thayer Mahan, a lecturer at the Naval War College in Newport, Rhode Island, published *The Influence of Sea Power upon History.* Someday someone should write a book entitled *The Influence upon History of The Influence of Sea Power upon History,* because no book had a greater effect on Hawaii's fate, except perhaps for *Memoirs of Henry Obookiah.*

Mahan's premise was that national greatness depended on sea power — a mighty navy, a robust merchant marine, global commerce, and, in the age of steam, strategically placed insular naval coaling stations. He included case studies on the wielding of naval power by the empires of Rome and Britain.

Mahan had befriended Theodore Roosevelt when he invited the young New Yorker to be a guest lecturer at the Naval War College because Roosevelt had written a book about the War of 1812.

Roosevelt's lust for naval dominance jibed with Mahan's own. "It is folly for the great English-speaking Republic to rely for defence upon a navy composed partly of antiquated hulks, and partly of new vessels rather more worthless than the old," he wrote.

Roosevelt would soon be appointed assistant secretary of the Navy. He and his fellow Republican and best friend, Massachusetts senator Henry Cabot Lodge, helped spread Mahan's ideas through Washington's corridors of power, eventually turning his argument for an imperial navy into the policy of the United States.

In March of 1893, just as the new president, Grover Cleveland withdrew his predecessor's treaty to annex Hawaii from the Senate, Mahan published an article in *Forum* magazine titled "Hawaii and Our Future Sea Power." Hawaii, he wrote, "fixes the attention of the strategist." He calls the archipelago a location "of unique importance . . . powerfully influencing the commercial and military control of the Pacific." He concludes that "the American Republic must abandon her isolationist tradition and emulate England's rise to greatness through the acquisition of an overseas empire."

In a letter to his sister at the time, Roosevelt lumped in Cleveland's failure to snatch up the islands with procrastination over building a canal in Central America. He wrote, "It is a great misfortune that we have not annexed Hawaii, gone on with our navy, and started an interoceanic canal at Nicaragua."

In 1895, Senator Lodge gave a series of foreign policy speeches in the Senate in which he discussed naval power and the acquisition of Hawaii, bringing Mahan's ideas about expanding America's empire at sea into the congressional record. America's interests, he claimed, demanded Hawaiian annexation. On March 2, 1895, Lodge bellowed of Hawaii, "Those islands, even if they were populated by a low race of savages, even if they were desert rocks, would still be important to this country from their position. On that ground, and on that ground alone, we ought to control and possess them."

Hawaii was just the sort of outlying island Mahan had written that a great nation needs to refuel and resupply its navy. But Mahan had always linked commercial trade with military might as the two key components to world power. That the Hawaiian Islands "have a great commerce and fertile soil," argued Lodge, "merely adds to the desirability of our taking them. The main thing is that those islands lie there in the heart of the Pacific, the controlling point in the commerce of that great ocean."

Then, practically plagiarizing Mahan, Lodge continued: "The sea power has been one of the controlling forces in history. Without the sea power no nation has been really great." Further parroting Mahan, Lodge explained that "Sea power consists, in the first place, of a proper navy and a proper fleet; but in order to sustain a navy we must have suitable posts for naval stations, strong places where a navy can be protected and refurnished." He concludes, "If we are ever to build the Nicaraguan Canal, it would be folly to enter upon it if we were not prepared to take possession of those islands."

The Republican Party platform in 1896 included United States control of Hawaii and the construction of a Central American canal, also controlled by the U.S. The GOP also expressed sympathy for "the heroic battle of the Cuban patriots against cruelty and oppression" as well as favoring "the continued enlargement of the navy and a complete system of harbor and seacoast defenses."

Once the Republican William McKinley was elected, Lodge convinced the president-elect to hire his friend Roosevelt as assistant secretary of the Navy.

Meanwhile, Queen Liliuokalani, now released from her palace prison, traveled to the United States to lobby against annexation once again. On a train from California heading east, she marveled, "Here were thousands of acres of uncultivated, uninhabited, but rich and fertile lands. . . . Colonies and colonies could be established here. . . . And yet this great and powerful nation must go across two thousand miles of sea, and take from the poor Hawaiians their little spots in the broad Pacific." She had a point, but it doesn't take a graduate of the Naval War College to notice you can't exactly park a battleship in Denver.

In March of 1897 the queen attended William McKinley's inauguration in Washington. She wrote of the parade, "I saw and intensely enjoyed the grand procession."

I wonder what she would have thought if she had known, witnessing that inaugural parade, that 112 years later, the first Hawaiian-born president of the United States would be inaugurated and in his parade the marching band from Punahou School, his alma mater (and that of her enemies), would serenade the new president by playing a song she had written, "Aloha 'Oe."

Roosevelt, the new assistant secretary of the Navy, gave a Mahanian address at the Naval War College in Newport on June 2, 1897, calling for a great navy because "no national life is worth having if the nation is not willing, when the need shall arise, to stake everything on the supreme arbitrament of war, and to pour out its blood, its treasure, and tears like water rather than submit to the loss of honor and renown."

Two weeks later, McKinley, egged on by Roosevelt and Lodge, signed a treaty of annexation with three representatives of the Republic of Hawaii, one of whom was Lorrin Thurston. The president submitted the treaty to the Senate for ratification.

In the coming months, native Hawaiians rallied to the cause of defeating the treaty's passage. The Hawaiian patriotic clubs, Hui Aloha Aina for Women and Hui Aloha Aina for Men, began a mass petition drive, their members fanning out around the islands, calling meetings and gathering signatures to protest annexation.

Reporter Miriam Michelson of the *San Francisco Call* witnessed one such meeting in Hilo on the Big Island on September 22,

1897. Michelson described a speech given by one of the leaders of the movement, Emma Nawahi, widow of the recently deceased lawyer, legislator, and newspaperman Joseph Nawahi. Mrs. Nawahi addressed her countrymen, asking for their signatures. She said:

The United States is just — a land of liberty. The people there are the friends — the great friends of the weak. Let us tell them — let us show them that as they love their country and would suffer much before giving it up, so do we love our country, our Hawai'i, and pray that they do not take it from us.

Our one hope is in standing firm — shoulder to shoulder, heart to heart. The voice of the people is the voice of God. Surely that great country across the ocean must hear our cry. By uniting our voices the sound will be carried on so they must hear us.

They did. According to the National Archives, where the Hawaiian patriotic leagues' petitions are stored, they collected more than twenty thousand native signatures. Four Hawaiian delegates carried the petitions to Washington, D.C., and, along with Queen Liliuokalani, presented the documents to the U.S. Congress.

The queen submitted her own protest to the Senate, stating, "I declare such a treaty to be an act of wrong toward the native and part-native people of Hawaii . . . [and] an act of gross injustice to me."

The Hawaiians were successful in lobbying lawmakers to defeat the treaty. On February 27, 1898, the treaty was defeated in the Senate when only forty-six senators voted in its favor.

A couple of weeks before the annual Kamehameha Day celebration in 2010, I accompanied my friend Laurel, the ex-blackjack dealer/missionary descendant/researcher, to a meeting of the Hawaiian Independence Action Alliance Project organized by Lynette Cruz, an activist and professor at Hawaii Pacific University. This was the same group who marched down Ala Moana Boulevard on the fiftieth anniversary of statehood, carrying the signs that said "We Are Not Americans."

Cruz and her comrades were planning to commemorate the 1897 petitions by making hundreds of signs to display on the Iolani Palace lawn. Their goal was for each name on the petitions to get its own sign.

"We are here to honor our *kupuna* past,"

Cruz said, using the Hawaiian word for ancestors to describe the signers of the petitions. "It's not a protest. This protest was done already in 1897. We're going to honor them now for the protest they did in 1897, which was successful."

I joined the dozen or so people who showed up and were sitting around, assembling signs. It was very neighborly, everyone snacking on potluck food, reminiscing about past protests, generally just chatting and joking around.

I met a dapper older gentleman named Tane. When I asked him his last name, he said, "It's just one name. Professionally, I go by that name. I was a singer at sea."

He says that he used to be a performer and cruise director for the Matson cruise ships, that he used to sail around the world. I ask him if he knew Don Ho. He says he did. I ask him if he could outsing Don Ho.

"Well, nobody thought that he had an exceptional voice," he says, laughing. "There were a lot of singers during his time that had more beautiful voices, but he was more of an entertainer than a singer."

I ask him if he has ancestors who signed the petitions against annexation. He says he does and finds them in the photocopies of the petitions Professor Cruz brought with her. He finds the names of his great-grandmother, his great-grandmother's brother, and their uncle: Elena Mihilani, Moses Nahia, and Henry Maialoha.

It must be a nice feeling, I say, to know that the names are stored in the National Archives.

"Yes," he says. "This is why Congress rejected the treaty. And since the treaty was rejected, then McKinley and his little elites decided to go through the route of a joint resolution, which is not lawful."

After the treaty died, a dizzying series of events in 1898 allowed the annexationists to sneak in the acquisition of Hawaii. To wit, the Spanish-American War: on February 15, the battleship *Maine* exploded in Havana Harbor. Warmongers exploited the "attack" (which may have been an explosion resulting from an accidental fire on board) and the U.S. declared war on Spain in April, supposedly, according to President McKinley, "to put an end to the barbarities, bloodshed, starvation, and horrible miseries now existing [in Cuba]."

On May 1, Admiral George Dewey's Asiatic Squadron invaded the Spanish port of Manila in the Philippines. Dewey decimated the entire Spanish squadron in six hours. This victory, now nearly forgotten, was such a big deal at the time that the city of New York threw Dewey a big parade and erected a triumphal arch in his honor in Madison Square in 1899. Torn down in 1901, the only evidence left of the admiral and his arch is a bar called Dewey's on Fifth Avenue and Twenty-Fifth Street, which displays a replica of the arch behind the bar and a wall mural of the Battle of Manila Bay. When I talked my friend Sherm into having lunch with me there, he wondered, "Were all late-nineteenth-century naval battles really fought over big city sports-bar naming rights?"

Dewey's triumph in Manila's harbor and the subsequent struggle to subdue the Philippines exaggerated Hawaii's importance to America as a coaling station and potential naval base. The U.S. already had the rights to use Pearl Harbor to resupply its ships with coal but the imperialists who had been lusting after the islands for years used the war in the Philippines as a pretext for snatching all of Hawaii once and for all. In fact, two months before Dewey's victory, McKinley had already confided in an aide, "We need Hawaii just as much and a good deal more than we did California. It is manifest destiny."

On May 4, three days after the Battle of

Manila Bay, a joint resolution to annex Hawaii was introduced in the House of Representatives.

"A joint resolution," scholar Keanu Sai told me, "is normally what the Congress of the United States does to say, 'We recognize this day is Joe Blow Day.' " He's right. H.J. RES. 374, for example, was "A joint resolution authorizing the President to proclaim the week of April 1, through April 7, 1980, as 'National Mime Week.' "

The introduction of the flimsy, barely legal joint resolution as a way of getting around the fact that President McKinley could not have achieved a proper treaty of annexation because he didn't have enough votes in Congress revived the congressional debate over American imperialism. Most if not all of the legislators opposed to annexing Hawaii objected to inviting the islands into the American family because of the large population of native Hawaiians and Asian field-workers. South Dakota Senator Richard F. Pettigrew worried, "If we adopt the policy of acquiring tropical countries, where republics cannot live, we overturn the theory upon which this Government is established."

Representative James "Champ" Clark, Democrat of Missouri, spun a (to him) nightmare scenario in which annexing Hawaii would lead to Hawaiian statehood down the road. He asked, "How can we endure our shame when a Chinese Senator from Hawaii, with his pigtail hanging down his back, with his pagan joss in his hand, shall rise from his curule chair and in pigeon English proceed to chop logic with George Frisbie Hoar or Henry Cabot Lodge?" (As it happened, Hawaii's first senator after statehood in 1959 was Hiram Fong, an Oahu native of Chinese descent, though Fong had pretty much the exact same haircut as Barry Goldwater.)

On June 15, the House passed the annexation resolution, 209 to 91. That day, the group that would come to be called the Anti-Imperialist League held a meeting at Faneuil Hall in Boston "to protest against the Adoption of a so-called imperial policy by the United States." Boston attorney Moorfield Storey warned, "When Rome began her career of conquest, the Roman Republic began to decay. . . . Let us once govern any considerable body of men without their consent, and it is a question of time how soon this republic shares the fate of Rome."

Buried there in the Spanish-American War timeline, in between the surrender of the

Spanish colonial island of Guam to the United States on June 20 and the July 17 surrender of Santiago in Cuba (thanks in part to the Rough Riders, including Theodore Roosevelt, who resigned as assistant secretary of the Navy to volunteer as a soldier), the Senate passed, and McKinley signed, the joint resolution annexing Hawaii to the United States on July 6.

On August 12, peace with Spain was declared *and* a ceremony was held at Iolani Palace, where the American flag was raised and Sanford Dole was sworn in as governor of the new Territory of Hawaii.

Ex-president Grover Cleveland wrote to his old secretary of state, Richard Olney, complaining, "Hawaii is ours. As I look back upon the first step in this miserable business and as I contemplate the means used to complete this outrage, I am ashamed of the whole affair."

In 1900, William McKinley invited his former assistant secretary of the Navy, a newly minted war hero, to be his running mate. When McKinley was assassinated in 1901, Theodore Roosevelt became the president of the United States.

For annexing Hawaii, McKinley was memorialized in Honolulu by a statue. Sanford Dole presided over the statue's dedication in 1911. It's still standing in Honolulu on the lawn of McKinley High School, the alma mater, incidentally, of Hawaii's first senator, Hiram Fong. The bronze McKinley holds in his hand a rolled up paper engraved with the words "Treaty of Annexation" even though no such treaty exists.

Kekuni Blaisdell, the activist whose grand-mothers worked for Queen Liliuokalani, drove me over to McKinley High to look at the statue. Pointing to the words "Treaty of Annexation," Blaisdell shook his head and sighed. "The lie continues," he said.

Blaisdell told me that one of his grand-fathers, a ship's captain, worked for the company that laid the telegraph cable across the Pacific, maintaining the cable between the West Coast of the United States and Hawaii. When the cable linking Hawaii to the Philippines was complete, President Theodore Roosevelt was given the honor of transmitting the very first round-the-world message on July 4, 1903. He wished "a happy Independence Day to the U.S., its territories and properties."

In a speech Roosevelt delivered in Chicago in 1905, "The Strenuous Life," TR distilled his personal and political philosophy into an argument for "the law of strife." Address-ing his fellow Americans, Roosevelt proclaimed, "If we are to be a really great people, we must strive in good faith to play a great part in the world." Regarding the acquisitions of 1898, he said, "We cannot avoid the responsibilities that confront us in Hawaii, Cuba, Puerto Rico, and the Philippines." Furthermore,

The timid man, the lazy man, the man who distrusts his country, the over-civilized man, who has lost the great fighting, masterful virtues . . . all these, of course, shrink from seeing the nation undertake its new duties; shrink from seeing us build a navy and an army adequate to our needs; shrink from seeing us do our share of world's work, by bringing order out of chaos in the great, fair tropic islands from which the valor of our soldiers and sailors has driven the Spanish flag. These are the men who fear the strenuous life, who fear the only national life which is really worth leading.

The overcivilized sissies Roosevelt was complaining about, the men shrinking from the nation's "new duties," included the Anti-Imperialist League. In 1899, the Anti-Imperialist League issued its official platform calling for a return to the old-fangled virtues of the "land of Washington and Lincoln." The platform condemned the annexation of the Philippines, claiming the new colonial policy "seeks to extinguish the spirit of 1776 in those islands." The league, cribbing from the Declaration of Independence, proclaimed, "We maintain that governments derive their just powers from the consent of the governed."

On March 7, 1900, Henry Cabot Lodge delivered a speech in the Senate in which he took up the crucial question of whether or not the imperialist developments of 1898 were a betrayal of the ideals of 1776. "Our opponents put forward as their chief objection that we have robbed these people of their liberty . . . in defiance of the doctrine of the Declaration of Independence in regard to the consent of the governed."

The evil genius of Lodge's argument is that he bypasses the question of whether the United States has received the consent of the islanders now governed by smacking down the notion that consent of the governed is even possible. He exposes the two-faced irony of the Declaration, pointing out that a healthy percentage of English colonists circa 1776 were loyal to the British crown. "Did we ask their consent?" he said of the decision to sever ties with England. "Not at all."

Then, after mentioning the founders' obvious disenfranchisement of white women and inhabitants of African descent, Lodge calls Thomas Jefferson, the Declaration's author, "the greatest expansionist in our history" for negotiating the Louisiana Purchase. Lodge wonders, "Did he ask the consent of the thirty thousand white men at the mouth of the Mississippi, or of the Indians roaming over the wide expanse of the Louisiana Purchase? Such an idea never occurred to him for one moment. He took Louisiana without the consent of the governed, and he ruled it without the consent of the governed."

Lodge goes on to mention that after the Civil War, "we forced the Southern States back into the Union" without their say-so; that the U.S. bought Alaska from the Russians without asking the permission of anyone living there; and that in his home state of Massachusetts, women and children are disenfranchised, thus restricting registered voters to one fifth of the state's population — and only half of those registered voted in the last election.

In short, Lodge asserts, American government derived from the consent of the governed "has never existed."

I'm not sure what is more disturbing — that the annexation of the Philippines, along with Hawaii, Puerto Rico, and Guam in 1898 is a betrayal of the principle of self-government established in 1776 or Lodge's allegation that the principle of self-government was, is, and always will be a delusion.

Lodge even went so far as to claim that the question of whether it is constitutional for a "domestic and dependent nation" to be absorbed within the United States had been settled by the Supreme Court way back in 1832, when Chief Justice John Marshall declared, in *Worcester v. Georgia,* that the Cherokee were a sovereign nation within American boundaries. Of course, Lodge doesn't bother to mention that the executive branch failed to enforce that ruling when the president authorized the Trail of Tears.

When I was spending time with those Hawaiians whose ancestors signed the petitions against annexation that were sent to Congress, I couldn't help but think back to the fruitless petition the Cherokee also sent to Congress to protest their removal. "Our only fortress is the justice of our cause," said the petition signed by my ancestors.

Alas, having read the writings of Alfred Thayer Mahan, I know that a sturdier fortress than a just cause is an actual fortress.

In January 1899, Carl Schurz of the Anti-Imperialist League gave a speech in Chicago three weeks after Spain officially ceded to the United States the Philippines, Puerto Rico, and Guam. Schurz suggested that citizens should reread the farewell address George Washington delivered when his second presidential term was ending in 1796. Washington warned Americans of the dangers of meddling in foreign affairs. The old general cautioned his fellow citizens to "avoid the necessity of those overgrown military establishments which, under any form of government, are inauspicious to liberty, and which are to be regarded as particularly hostile to republican liberty."

Schurz shared this fear of militarism. Among his many worries about the colonial corner the country had just turned was exactly what Roosevelt, Lodge, and Mahan had called for: "a material increase of our army or navy" to protect the new island acquisitions against "any probable foreign attack that might be provoked by their being in our possession." Then, having predicted the Japanese attack on Pearl Harbor forty-two years later, Schurz prophesies the entire twentieth-century arms race. He fears that American armaments would be determined "by the armaments of their rivals" if someday, like the European empires, "We, too, shall nervously watch reports from abroad telling us that this power is augmenting the number of its warships, or that another is increasing its battalions . . . and we shall follow suit," eventually requiring "larger armies and navies than we now have."

As I write this, more than a century after Schurz gave that speech, Schurz's nightmares, and Alfred Thayer Mahan's dreams, have all come true. The American military installations in Hawaii alone include, besides the original object of military desire, Pearl Harbor Naval Base, Fort Ruger, Fort Shafter, Hickham Air Force Base, Marine Corps Base Hawaii, Pacific Missile Range Facility, Pohakuloa Training Area, Schofield Barracks, and Wheeler Air Force Base, as well as the headquarters of the United States Pacific Command, whose self-proclaimed "Area of Responsibility (AOR) encompasses about half the earth's surface, stretching from the waters off the west coast of the U.S. to the western border of India, and from Antarctica to the North Pole."

■ ■ ■ ■

One Memorial Day, I went up to Honolulu's National Memorial Cemetery of the Pacific. More than 30,000 American casualties from World War II and the wars in Korea and Vietnam are buried there in the Punchbowl volcanic crater.

The Hawaiians call Punchbowl *Puowaina,* meaning "Hill of Sacrifice," for it is thought that back during the kapu system, men and women who had been executed for violating the kapu were taken up to Punchbowl, where their bodies were cremated. Once Kamehameha established the monarchy, he mounted his cannons on the crater's rim, firing them off on ceremonial occasions. It's also the hill Hiram Bingham climbed on his first day in Honolulu in 1820, the place he stood surveying his new home, marveling at the ocean and Diamond Head before him, feeling like Moses gazing upon the Promised Land, spying what had been the "battle-field of . . . the last victory of Kamehameha" and vowing "it was now to be the scene of a bloodless conquest for Christ."

Congress provided funding to build a military cemetery in 1948. It is filled to capacity. On Memorial Day, each grave is decorated with an American flag. That is the fruit of Alfred Mahan's ideas and Theodore Roosevelt's ideals — 30,000 American flags flapping in the wind above American remains in the crater of an extinct Polynesian volcano.

At Punchbowl's Memorial Day service, after a speech by Hawaii's senator, the Japanese-American World War II veteran (and McKinley High alumnus) Daniel Inouye, after performances of "Amazing Grace" and taps, the national anthem and "God Bless America," after the Hickham Air Force Honor Guard shot a twenty-one-gun salute and the Hawaii Air National Guard's 199th Fighter Squadron flew over our heads in the Missing Man formation, then the Royal Hawaiian Band, the Pearl City High School Choir, and the Honolulu Boy Choir joined together to play and sing "Hawaii Pono'i," Hawaii's state song. It was written by King David Kalakaua as a hymn to the power of King Kamehameha the Great: Na kaua e pale/Me ka ihe (Who guarded in the war/With his spear).

After the ceremony, I took a seat on one of the buses that were waiting to take attendees back downtown. Big American flags slapped the windows as we pulled away from the cemetery and I thought about another, sadder, song about Kamehameha I heard one morning on the island of Lanai.

I was eating breakfast with my sister Amy and nephew Owen at a Four Seasons resort. Not the Four Seasons at the beach, the one done up in "Hawaiian-Polynesian-Mediterranean styles with an Asian influence." We were at the Four Seasons in the Lanai hills decorated, for some reason, like an old English country estate. We had walked up there from Lanai City to see an old Norfolk Island pine tree, a gift from King David Kalakaua to Walter Murray Gibson that locals saved from the resort's bulldozers by raising a stink.

So we were sitting there on the set of *Brideshead Revisited* eating eggs and Portuguese sausages and the song "Hawaii '78" starts playing in the background. Before the singer breaks into English, he wails something in Hawaiian. I can pick out *'aina,* the word for land.

Owen asked, "Is this Iz?"

I might have marveled that this blond, blue-eyed eight-year-old mainlander — Baby Custer I used to call him — recognizes the voice of the late Hawaiian crooner Israel Kamakawiwo'ole, affectionately nicknamed Iz. But it wasn't Owen's first trip to Hawaii. Anyone who has been to any of the islands for more than fifteen minutes and hasn't heard Iz's cover of "Over the Rainbow" at least five times is not paying attention. In fact, on Owen's first trip to Hawaii, when I took him to the Big Island to cheer him up after he was diagnosed with the family wheat allergy my sister and I enjoy, the three of us were in line at a seaside resort's breakfast buffet, undoubtedly steering clear of the pastry selection, when the opening ukulele chords of Iz's "Over the Rainbow" came on the PA system just as it had every other time we left our room. A man behind us in line sighed noisily, complaining, "If I had a dollar for every time I heard this song in Hawaii, I could afford to stay another night in this damn hotel."

"Over the Rainbow" is as sweet and soft as trade winds rustling through palms. It is the perfect song for Hawaiian vacations because the tranquility of its sound captures the feeling tourists flock there to find. Even though it's a song that is actually about the human inability to be happy where one is, the suspicion that joy is always somewhere else. It is not unlike the hymns the New England missionaries brought to Hawaii, advertisements for heaven, that other elusive elsewhere where troubles melt like lemondrops. The trick of Iz's tender arrangement of the song is how convincing a case he makes that finally, and for once, You Are Here.

In "Hawaii '78," on the other hand, Iz confronts the price of that dreamy little swindle. Storm clouds gather over a crowded city, unless those are exhaust fumes. He wonders what Kamehameha the Great would think of his kingdom being mucked up with highways and condominiums. "Cry for the land," Iz moans. Earnest and mournful, as if singing from the bizarro B side of "Over the Rainbow," in "Hawaii '78" he reaches an opposite conclusion: "Our land is in great, great danger now."

"What is this song about?" Owen wondered.

"It's about how people like us wrecked this place," I say. Then the Filipina waitress came by and asked him if he would like more juice.

Still, the song is not only about that. Iz's teary list of all the tacky changes that would bring tears to the eyes of the old warrior king concludes, "And then yet you'll find Hawaii." Which is true. Hawaii can still be found: in the swaying hips of high school students performing hula dances down the hill from David Malo's grave; in the arms of men rowing an outrigger canoe below the cave where Queen Kaahumanu was born; in the fingertip of an old man pointing to his ancestors' names on an antique petition; and every time two Hawaiians really say hello, touching noses, breathing each other in.

ACKNOWLEDGMENTS

I would like to thank: my old pal and taskmaster Geoffrey Kloske at Riverhead Books, along with his colleagues Laura Perciasepe, Mih-Ho Cha, Craig Burke, and Susan Petersen Kennedy; David Levinthal for his cover photograph; Steven Barclay and Sara Bixler at Steven Barclay Agency; Jaime Wolf at Pelosi, Wolf, Effron & Spates; Elisa Shokoff at Simon & Schuster Audio; Ted Thompson and Anthony Mascorro for transcribing interview tapes; John Cheever, Ira Glass, Mark Maretzski, and John-Mario Sevilla for reading drafts of the book; and especially Amy Vowell and Owen Brooker for their company in the islands. Also, Jack Alexander, Eric Bogosian, Bill Heinzen, Michael Giacchino, Nick Hornby, Damon Lindelof, Greil Marcus, Jenny Marcus, Bennett Miller, Jim Nelson, Jonathan Marc Sherman, Pat and Janie Vowell, and Wendy Weil. For their help and/or hospitality in Hawaii:

the archivists at the Bishop Museum Archives, the archivists at Hawaii State Archives, Kekuni Blaisdell, Leimana Brimeyer, the bus drivers of Honolulu, Lynette Cruz, Barbara Dunn at the Hawaiian Historical Society, Tim Dyke, Guy Gaumont, Margaret Hamamoto, Paul Hamamoto, Hawaiian Independence Action Alliance, Lori Gomez-Karinen at Lahainaluna High School, Noelle Kahanu at the Bishop Museum, Ken Kimura of the Lahaina Restoration Foundations, Gaylord Kubota, Kepa Maly at Lanai Culture & Heritage Center, Barbara Morgan and Carlyn Tani at Punahou School, Keanu Sai, Mike Smola at Mission Houses Museum, and Carol White at Mission Houses Museum Library and Archives. I am especially grateful to Laurel "Seeti" Douglass for sharing her knowledge, enthusiasm, and time.

BIBLIOGRAPHY

*recommended reading

Jacob Adler, *Claus Spreckels: The Sugar King in Hawaii,* 1966.

Jacob Adler, *The Fantastic Life of Walter Murray Gibson,* 1986.

Helena G. Allen, *Sanford Ballard Dole, Hawaii's Only President,* 1988.

Rufus Anderson, *History of the Sandwich Islands Mission,* 1870.

Hiram Bingham, *A Residence of Twenty-One Years in the Sandwich Islands,* 1847.

Isabella L. Bird, *The Hawaiian Archipelago,* 1875.*

Lady Maria Callcott, et al., *Voyage of H.M.S. Blonde to the Sandwich Islands,* 1826.

Helen Geracimos Chapin, *Shaping History: The Role of Newspapers in Hawaii,* 1996.*

John Charlot, "The Feather Skirt of Nahi'ena'ena: An Innovation in Postcontact Hawaiian Art," *The Journal of the Polynesian Society* 100, no. 2 (1991).*

Tom Coffman, *Nation Within,* 1998.*

Robert Dampier, *To the Sandwich Islands on the H.M.S. Blonde,* 1971.

Gavan Daws, *A Dream of Islands,* 1980.*

Gavan Daws, *Shoal of Time,* 1986.*

Sanford B. Dole and Lorrin A. Thurston, *Memoirs of the Hawaiian Revolution,* 1936.

Eric Jay Dolin, *Leviathan: The History of Whaling in America,* 2007.*

Edwin Dwight, *Memoirs of Henry Obookiah,* 1819.

Walter Murray Gibson, *The Diaries of Walter Murray Gibson,* 1973.

John Dominis Holt, *On Being Hawaiian,* 1964.*

Piilani Kaluaikoolau, *The True Story of Kaluaikoolau,* 2001.

Samuel M. Kamakau, *Ruling Chiefs of Hawaii,* 1992.

Ralph Kuykendall, *The Hawaiian Kingdom: 1778–1854,* 1938.

Ralph Kuykendall, *The Hawaiian Kingdom: 1854–1874,* 1938.

Ralph Kuykendall, *The Hawaiian Kingdom: 1874–1893,* 1953.

Liliuokalani, *Hawaii's Story by Hawaii's Queen,* 1898.*

Henry Cabot Lodge, *Speeches and Addresses, 1884–1909,* 1909.

David Malo, *Hawaiian Antiquities,* 1987.

Alfred Thayer Mahan, "Hawaii and Our Future Sea Power," *The Forum,* March 1893.

Alfred Thayer Mahan, *The Influence of Sea Power Upon History, 1660–1783,* 1890.*

Frederick Merk, *Manifest Destiny and Mission in American History,* 1963.

Thomas J. Osborne, *Empire Can Wait: American Opposition to Hawaiian Annexation, 1893–1898,* 1981.*

Jonathan K. Osorio, *Dismembering Lahui,* 2002.*

Nathaniel Philbrick, *Sea of Glory,* 2003.*

Mary Kawena Pukui and Samuel H. Elbert, editors, *Hawaiian Dictionary,* 1986.

Mary A. Richards, *The Hawaiian Chiefs' Children's School,* 1970.

Robert C. Schmitt and Eleanor C. Nordyke, "Death in Hawai'i: The Epidemics of 1848–1849," *The Hawaiian Journal of History,* volume 35, 2001.*

Noenoe K. Silva, *Aloha Betrayed,* 2004.*

Cummins E. Speakman, Jr., *Mowee: An Informal History of the Hawaiian Island,* 1978.

Robert H. Stauffer, *Kahana: How the Land*

Was Lost, 2003.*

Ronald T. Takaki, *Pau Hana,* 1986.*

Nicholas Thomas, *Cook,* 2003.

William Henry Thomes, *A Whaleman's Adventures in the Sandwich Islands and California,* 1890.

Lucy Goodale Thurston, *Life and Times of Mrs. Lucy G. Thurston,* 1882.

Jon M. Van Dyke, *Who Owns the Crown Lands of Hawaii?,* 2007.*

Carol Wilcox, *Sugar Water,* 1998.*

Charles Wilkes, *Narrative of the United States Exploring Expedition,* 1845.

Mary Zwiep, *Pilgrim Path,* 1991.

ABOUT THE AUTHOR

Sarah Vowell is the bestselling author of *The Wordy Shipmates, Assassination Vacation, The Partly Cloudy Patriot, Take the Cannoli,* and *Radio On.* She lives in New York City.